BEER
Craft

SIX-PACKS
from
SCRATCH

D0122042

A SIMPLE GUIDE TO MAKING GREAT BEER

BEER
Craft

WILLIAM BOSTWICK AND JESSI RYMILL

RODALE

CONTENTS

2

Make

PLUS Inside tips from the brewers at . . . AVERY, THE BRUERY, GREAT DIVIDE, LAGUNITAS, TRÖEGS, *AND MORE!*

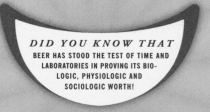

DID YOU KNOW THAT
BEER HAS STOOD THE TEST OF TIME AND
LABORATORIES IN PROVING ITS BIO-
LOGIC, PHYSIOLOGIC AND
SOCIOLOGIC WORTH!

Bottle neck label, Koppitz Pale Select Beer,
Koppitz-Melchers Brewery, Detroit, c. 1936

Forget everything you know about homebrewing.

If you're like us when we started, that'll be easy—we didn't know anything. If you like making things, love beer, and aren't afraid to get your hands dirty or mess up the kitchen a bit, you can make the best beer you've ever tasted, right on your stove. It doesn't cost much, and it doesn't take very long—an afternoon in the kitchen and a week waiting for it to ferment. In fact, the hardest part of making beer is being patient.

We're not professionals. For us, brewing beer is a passion and a hobby. There are dozens of ways to make beer—after all, people have been doing it for 12,000 years. We've tried most of them, and have gotten advice from homebrewers and craft brewers who've tried the rest. We know what works and what doesn't, and we've saved enough trophy bottles (and dumped enough bad batches) to prove it.

We brew on a budget, in a tiny apartment kitchen, without any fancy equipment. We brew from scratch, with all-natural whole grains instead of canned extracts. We like inventing our own recipes. And we brew in small, one-gallon batches—they're quick, easy to experiment with, and they actually fit on our stovetop.

Brewing beer doesn't have to be complicated. We make the process easy and keep the recipes basic so you can focus on more important things, like finding out what makes a dark, toasty porter so delicious, or how to get a spicy winter ale just the way you like it (in our case, extra licorice, and hold the vanilla). You'll learn the history of your favorite beer styles, how to design labels for your bottles, and how to pair your homebrew with food. You'll meet the brewers driving the craft beer movement and get their advice on adventurous techniques like barrel-aging and dry-hopping.

This is a guide to homebrewing as we see it, with all the cheap tricks, secret shortcuts, and what-ifs that make it so exciting. Try it our way, or just use us as inspiration. No matter what, you'll make the best beer in the world—your own.

A DROP IN THE BARREL

The standard unit of measurement for beer is the barrel. In America, that's 31 gallons; in Britain, it's 36 imperial gallons (about 43 U.S. gallons). Of course, few American breweries store beer in barrels (or in hogsheads, tierces, kilderkins, or other innumerable and curious subsets), preferring instead the keg. You'll make yours by the gallon, but be sure not to brew more than 200 batches per year, or else you'll be sharing a pint with the Feds—it's illegal to make that much untaxed booze.

1 BARREL
(2 KEGS)

1 KEG
(15 ½ GALLONS)

1 GALLON
(10 ⅔ BOTTLES)

Beer History

For the first 150 years of American history, beer was made at home, using methods practically unchanged since the Sumerians. Then, in only a few decades in the 19th century, Pabst turned from a start-up into the biggest, most advanced brewery in the world.

Cheap adjuncts like corn and rice were the saviors of American beer before they became its scourges. Light beer was invented 5,000 years ago but flooded American bars in the span of only five. The story of beer is the story of traditions that never change—until they suddenly, and profoundly, do.

Beer began, as do all great things, as a happy accident—a gift from the gods. About 12,000 years ago, somewhere in the rolling fertile hills of the Middle East, a lucky Mesopotamian found beer. Cereal grains were being harvested for the first time, and maybe a stockpile got wet, baked in the sun, was rained on again, and a curious farmer slurped up some of the runoff. Or maybe a baker munched on a loaf of old, fermented bread. We don't really know how it was first discovered. But we do know that a few thousand years later, beer had become a staple of the planet's first civilizations.

Pictograms from 4000 BC show pairs of drinkers draining enormous jars through long, bent straws. By 3000 BC, Mesopotamians had recorded recipes for more than 20 different kinds of beer, with names like "beer to sniff" and "lessens the waist" (presumably the first light beer). In fact, writing itself probably emerged as a way to keep track of stored grain and the beer made from it—an early form of currency. According to the first recorded laws, the Code of Hammurabi, beer rations were a legal right. Sumerian temple workers were paid a liter a day; pyramid builders in Giza got eight.

But beer was bigger than economics. As humans quit their nomadic runaround and settled into cities, beer offered a sanitary alternative to communal—that is, often polluted—drinking water, plus the protein and vitamin B that early humans missed once their diet moved from meat to grain. Not that they knew that. To the world's first drinkers, beer was magic. Fermentation wouldn't be completely understood until the 18th century. Until then, it was the domain of gods like Hathor and Ninkasi.

The Greeks and Romans learned about beer from the Egyptians (in fact, the word "beer" comes from the Latin *bibere,* to drink) but soon moved on to wine, leaving beer to the uncivilized hordes. Germanic and British tribes like the Picts were already brewing by the time the legions showed up, tossing in honey and heather flowers—to Caesar and

12,000 YEARS OF BEER HISTORY

10,000 BC Nomadic man settles down, starts farming grain in Mesopotamia

4300 BC Sumerians scribble the world's oldest recipe on cuneiform clay tablets: beer made from twice-baked barley cakes

| 10,000 BC | 9000 BC | 8000 BC | 7000 BC | 6000 BC | 5000 BC |

his soldiers, just another sign of barbarism. The "horrible brew," Gaius Cornelius Tacitus snickered, had "a very far removed similarity to wine."

While grapevines slowly blanketed southern Europe, those "barbarians" were refining brewing to an art that, once established in the Dark Ages, barely changed until the 1840s. Hops didn't show up until AD 1000, when Bremen brewers in Germany used them to preserve ale that was being carried along the burgeoning inter-European trade routes. Before then, brewers flavored beer with a mix of spices called gruit. Each town had its own unique blend, doled out by the local church or government, but gruit generally contained bitter, piney herbs, such as bog myrtle and wild rosemary, juniper, anise, nutmeg, and caraway.

With Romans out of the way by the first millennium, monasteries provided Europe with order, and with beer—monks were allowed to drink on the Sabbath. *"Liquida non frangunt ienium,"* they said: Liquid doesn't break the fast. As the church's power waned, brewing was dispersed to guilds. Before 1300, towns had as many breweries as they had monasteries. By 1500, Hamburg alone had more than 600 breweries. Brewing was now a business. Beer was traded and laws were made. Germany's Reinheitsgebot, which allowed only certain ingredients in beer, was first signed in 1516—and still holds today. Bavaria banned summer brewing (thought to be unhealthy), limiting production to the winter, and the lagers they're still famous for. Regional styles became brands.

Meanwhile, when King Henry VIII shut down England's monasteries

Rule of Three

Duke Wilhelm IV of Bavaria imposed the Reinheitsgebot, or beer purity law, in 1516, limiting all beer made in Germany to three ingredients: barley, hops, and water (no one knew about yeast yet). The law probably had nothing to do with quality, and was more an effort by the Duke to control the barley trade. When Otto von Bismarck unified Germany in 1871, he required the new northern states to sign the law, and dozens of weird regional styles like the oatmeal-honey-and-molasses Kotbüsser went underground. European courts repealed the law in 1987, but Germany reinstated a slightly looser version of it in 1993. Yeast and pure sugars, okay; molasses and honey, still *verboten*.

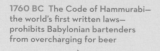

1760 BC The Code of Hammurabi— the world's first written laws— prohibits Babylonian bartenders from overcharging for beer

50 BC Roman legions taste Germanic beer, but stick with wine

AD 1 Barrels are invented, bringing long-term storage, and stale beer

600 Romans leave Europe, monks begin brewing

3000 BC   2000 BC   1000 BC   AD 1   500   1000

in 1536, he didn't shut down brewing—monks just stayed on their redistributed land and made beer at their new landlords' houses, or commercially. Hops were arriving from Flanders around then, and British beers became, on the whole, brown, smoky, and bitter. They went bad often. These were not good days for beer.

Tavern-goers took to cutting sour beer with newer batches, and porter was born. With it came industrialized brewing. By 1796, one London brewery was making 202,000 36-gallon barrels of porter a year. In 1810, Londoners brewed and drank more than a million barrels of the stuff.

This was the beer colonial Americans were used to. Pale ale was a high-class drink back in England, available to those who could afford the more expensive coal-kilned malts, and the glass mugs to appreciate its color (think the officer corps in the British Indian Army). Pale ale was great, porter would do fine, but the earliest settlers couldn't even get a mug of sour brown. Thomas Studly complained from Jamestown that "there remained neither taverne, beer house, nor place of relief." England did what it could. John Winthrop rode in on a ship heavy with 10,000 gallons of beer, but most of it spoiled on the way over—or was finished off by the sailors. Americans had to fend for themselves. Even Winthrop brewed his own.

Unfortunately, grains didn't grow too well in the New World, and hops were a hassle, so settlers used everything else: corn, spruce tips, maple sap, pumpkins, apples, persimmons, even parsnips. A recipe from

1500 Church loses grip on gruit, hops take over brewing

1516 Bavarians enact Reinheitsgebot

1722 First true porter brewed in England

AD 1450   1500   1550   1600   1650   1700

Providence, Rhode Island, for a beer "famous throughout the country-side" called for one ounce of senna leaves, chicory, or celandine, and one handful of red sage boiled in 10 quarts of water with wheat bran, a quart of molasses, and a quart of malt.

Thomas Jefferson thought the best beer was made by winging it: "I have no receipt [recipe] for brewing and I doubt if the operations of malting and brewing can be successfully performed from a receipt." This was experimental stuff, but even so, the average American in the 1790s drank 34 gallons of beer a year. (Today it's a bit over half of that.) Almost every home had a brew pot. Bad beer was better than no beer.

By the end of the 18th century, rum—cheap and strong—began to dominate taverns and to mellow that first great wave of American experimentation with beer. By the early 1800s, American beer was dead. But when 1.2 million Germans immigrated to the United States in the 1840s, they brought their beer culture with them, and it quickly took over. The breweries they built—40 in Philadelphia that decade alone—made one thing only: lager. Gone were the pumpkin ales and spiced beers of the 1700s. Temperance movements cut annual beer consumption to only three gallons per person in 1840, and most of that was lager. The style was put on trial in 1858 when a Brooklyn brewer was arrested for drinking on Sunday. Lager was found not guilty, and America found its national drink.

One of the biggest surprises in American beer history is how little

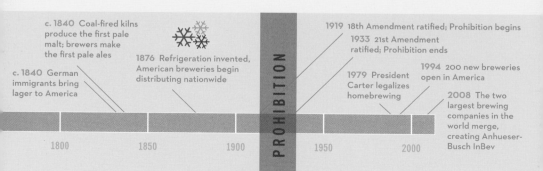

c. 1840 Coal-fired kilns produce the first pale malt; brewers make the first pale ales

c. 1840 German immigrants bring lager to America

1876 Refrigeration invented, American breweries begin distributing nationwide

PROHIBITION

1919 18th Amendment ratified; Prohibition begins

1933 21st Amendment ratified; Prohibition ends

1979 President Carter legalizes homebrewing

1994 200 new breweries open in America

2008 The two largest brewing companies in the world merge, creating Anhueser-Busch InBev

1800   1850   1900   1950   2000

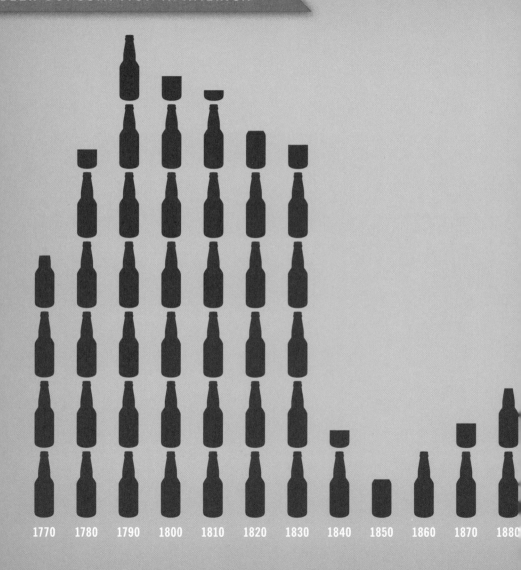

1770 1780 1790 1800 1810 1820 1830 1840 1850 1860 1870 1880

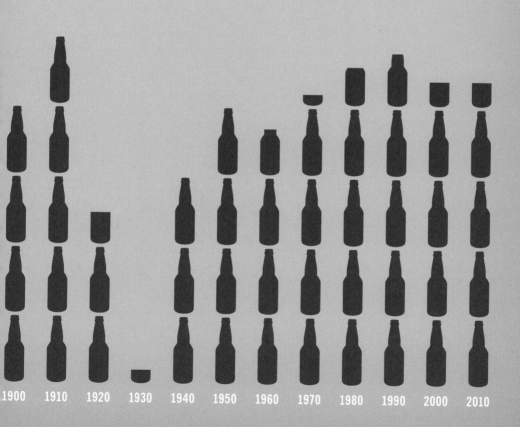

A BOTTLE A DAY...

This graph shows the amount of beer—measured in bottles per week—downed by the average American in each decade. Beer drinking peaked in the 18th century, started to decline as rum got popular, and was practically destroyed in the 1840s by a mixture of temperance and anti-German xenophobia. It had only just recovered when Prohibition struck. Today, we drink about as much beer as we did during the Revolutionary War.

1900 1910 1920 1930 1940 1950 1960 1970 1980 1990 2000 2010

our national taste has changed in 150 years. Light lagers then—as they are now—were considered cleaner, more refreshing, and healthier than the darker, spicier, heavier beers the British first brought with them. In fact, Anheuser-Busch, Pabst, and other early lager brewers started thinning their beers with rice and corn (by then an agricultural product far removed from the Indian corn that Jefferson and Winthrop used) as early as the 1870s. These blander grains made beer brewed from protein-rich American 6-row barley taste more like the paler pils the Germans brewed back home.

In the 19th century, big brewers got even bigger. Yeast was better understood, methods for measuring and fine-tuning alcohol content were developed, refrigeration was invented, and brewing became a science—and big business. Anheuser-Busch, Miller, and Pabst shipped their beer in refrigerated rail cars all over the country. They owned bars on every major corner in the country. Pabst became the biggest brewery in the world in the early 1890s, the first to sell one million barrels a year. Budweiser and Miller weren't far behind. Prices fell, production rose, and smaller breweries were left in the lurch. There were more than 4,000 breweries in America in 1870; by 1910 that number was down to 1,500.

Prohibition was the last straw. What began as a way to stamp out saloons—and the whoring and gambling that went on inside them—soon became an attack on beer itself, as the new temperance movement merged with a fear of factories and industrial food. Mass-produced beers were a step away from *The Jungle*'s canned meats. The 16th Amendment set up the income tax, which overtook the tax on beer as the government's main revenue source, and left breweries out in the cold when Prohibition hit. Most never recovered.

Some breweries managed to stay afloat during those 13 long years—Yuengling sold ice cream, Budweiser sold soda, others sold yeast to bakers. A few tried marketing extra-low-alcohol "near beer," but watery slop like Budweiser's Bevo never caught on. The Depression and a hooch-soaked crime wave set the government backpedaling, and beer was again put on trial. In 1933, beer at or under 3.2 percent ABV (alcohol

American Lager

Before badass IPAs and bourbon-barrel stouts, American brewing was known for one thing: lager. Cut with rice and corn to mimic the crystal-clear Czech pilsners so popular in Europe, American lagers developed a style all their own. Today, mass-market beer can be more than a quarter adjunct grain, lightly flavored with extracts and oils. It's served ice-cold—the better to numb the taste buds—and it's the most popular beer in the U.S. Or rather, it was, until the light versions came out. Today's ranking: Bud Lite, Miller Lite, Budweiser, Coors Light.

by volume) was found "non-intoxicating," and Prohibition was over. But the rise of powerful cocktails and cheap, sugary soda as Depression-friendly ways to an easy buzz meant that a year after Prohibition ended, demand for beer was only half of the 80 million barrels breweries could produce.

Few breweries survived. Those that did just grew bigger, as a brand-new highway system helped them spread their fizzy wares—now in easy-to-ship cans—from sea to shining sea. Women began buying beer, and men began drinking it at home. By 1945, two-thirds of all beer sold was packaged; before Prohibition, two-thirds had been sold on draft. Beer entered grocery stores for the first time, since breweries no longer held sway over bars, and that meant a new focus on advertising and distribution. Whoever reached the most customers won. The '70s brought a diet craze to a post-Depression generation raised on sugar and soda, and Miller invented a light beer in 1975. Two years later, there were 19 more. Schlitz was pumping its beer full of silica gel, corn syrup, and hop extracts, looking to save a buck. Miller, bloated on cash from its new owner, Philip-Morris, scooped up the last few remaining small breweries like Wisconsin's beloved Leinenkugel. By 1978 there were only 41 brewing companies in the country.

Beer was barely breathing. In an infamous 1973 column in the *Chicago Tribune*, Mike Royko fired the first rebel shot: American beer "tastes as if the secret brewing process involved running it through a horse." Michael Jackson's *World Guide to Beer* came out in 1977 and threw into relief what the nation was missing. The hunt was on for something better. The *New York Times* started praising the little guys: Yuengling, Iron City, Koehlers. *Esquire* filed their "First-Ever American Regional Beer Survey," passing over Bud for local gems like Pickett's Premium of Dubuque, Iowa.

Things started changing. In 1974, Byron Burch spent $5,000 to self-publish *Quality Brewing: A Guidebook for the Home Production of Fine Beers* out of his Berkeley, California, wine-making shop. The first home-brewing club opened in Los Angeles that year, making beer-pun history: the Maltose Falcons. Four years later, President Jimmy Carter legalized

Learn the Craft

The Brewers Association has strict rules about what counts as craft beer. First, a craft brewery can't make more than two million barrels of beer per year (a microbrewery produces 15,000 barrels or less). Second, that beer has to be all-barley, with any extra grain used only to enhance flavor, not lighten it. And finally, at least 75 percent of the brewery must be independently owned by a brewer—not a corporation.

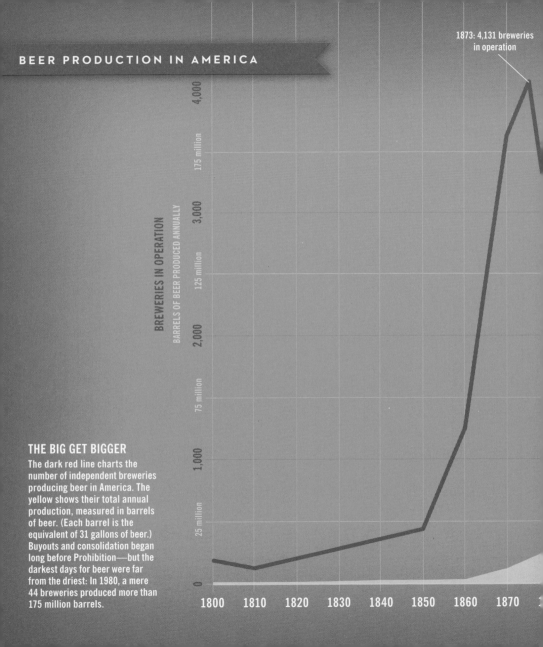

BEER PRODUCTION IN AMERICA

BREWERIES IN OPERATION
BARRELS OF BEER PRODUCED ANNUALLY

1873: 4,131 breweries in operation

THE BIG GET BIGGER
The dark red line charts the number of independent breweries producing beer in America. The yellow shows their total annual production, measured in barrels of beer. (Each barrel is the equivalent of 31 gallons of beer.) Buyouts and consolidation began long before Prohibition—but the darkest days for beer were far from the driest: In 1980, a mere 44 breweries produced more than 175 million barrels.

4,000

3,000

2,000

1,000

175 million

125 million

75 million

25 million

1800 1810 1820 1830 1840 1850 1860 1870

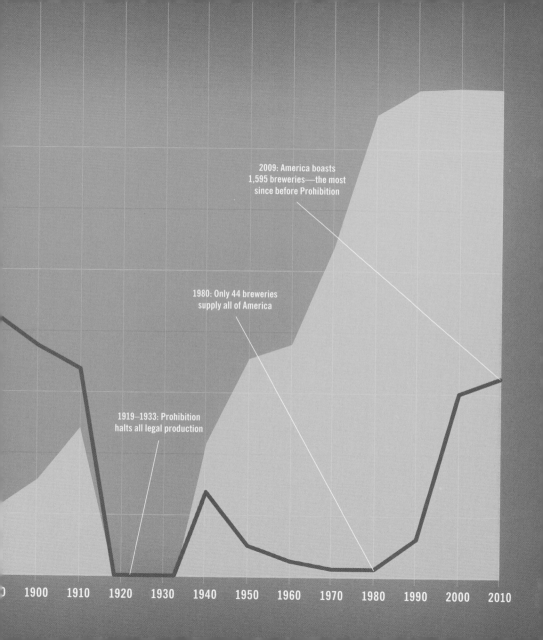

2009: America boasts
1,595 breweries—the most
since before Prohibition

1980: Only 44 breweries
supply all of America

1919–1933: Prohibition
halts all legal production

1900 1910 1920 1930 1940 1950 1960 1970 1980 1990 2000 2010

homebrewing, and Charlie Papazian and Charlie Matzen launched the American Homebrewers Association.

And the changes weren't happening only at home. In 1976, Jack McAuliffe fired up a scrapped-together 45-gallon vat in Sonoma, California, and made the first New Albion ale. In 1979, Fritz Maytag installed copper kettles and stainless-steel pipes in the new home for Anchor Brewing—and the company's nearly extinct Steam beer—moving from the 150-year-old rust trap he'd bought 10 years earlier. Around that same time, Ken Grossman and Paul Camusi pooled $50,000 to open Sierra Nevada. It took them 11 failed batches to settle on a recipe for their Pale Ale, but by 2000 they were the ninth largest brewery in the country. Jim Koch did for lagers what Anchor did for a forgotten ale, brewing the first Sam Adams in 1985; in 1987, Ronald Reagan had one at the White House.

If anything, American craft beer boomed too fast. More than 200 breweries opened between 1993 and 1994, doubling the country's output of small-batch beer. It was too much of the same thing. How many pale-wheat-stout breweries with leafy-green labels can a country handle? Breweries started closing their taps after having opened them just a few years before. Unless, of course, they specialized.

Soon, and again by necessity, American brewing began to find its voice, looking back past Bud, Bavaria, and Britain and reclaiming the spirit of its earliest brewing days, inventing its own styles, bold and ballsy. Dogfish Head egged on drinkers craving the exact opposite of mild lagers with some of the hoppiest—and most alcoholic—beers around, using four times as much malt and far more elaborate hop-dosing systems than bigger, more cost-conscious breweries would dare to try. Founders Brewing rebranded with a strong Scottish-style ale as its flagship, Dirty Bastard. Stone Brewing launched in 1996 with Arrogant Bastard. Its logo: a menacing gargoyle. Its tagline: "You're not worthy." Avery, another early-'90s brewery facing the threat of extinction by commonality, switched gears by brewing Hog Heaven, an extra-bitter, extra-strong so-called Imperial Red Ale. Or was it a barleywine? Made-up styles were hardly out-of-bounds for this new wave of brewers. Meanwhile, Jeff Lebesch snuck a few bottles of Belgian beer back to Colorado, cultivated their yeast, and introduced America to Abbey Ales. (Strangely enough, the style was fairly new even in Belgium—strong Trappist beers were a mid-20th-century invention aimed at kick-starting a flagging Belgian economy with a new sense of beery independence.)

Hops, which once had been one of the country's major crops (New York state alone harvested 60 million pounds in 1879), began sprouting up on the West Coast, fueling a gold rush for bitterer and bitterer beers. Citrusy IPAs, Double IPAs, Imperial IPAs: These became America's new beer identity.

They still are, to an extent—though the extra-bitter-IPA brewery of today is becoming what the pale-wheat-stout brewery was to the '90s, and the latest wave of craft brewing is exploring new territory. Breweries like Russian River, Jolly Pumpkin, and Firestone Walker are mining Belgian beer and American wine and whiskey traditions for inspiration. Strong beer still sells, but subtlety and sourness are gaining ground.

Still, craft beer makes up only about 4 percent of the total American beer market by volume. Craft sales keep going up—9 percent in 2009, 12 percent in 2010—but Budweiser (now part of InBev), Miller, and Coors (now joined as MillerCoors) still dominate. Is there hope for craft beer? Consider this: Ninety percent of Americans live within 10 miles of a craft brewery. Even closer if they're homebrewers. In the face of the seemingly unstoppable march of the big guys, it helps to remember that beer history is cyclical. Temperance movements rise and, thankfully, fall. Craft beer's renaissance is just that: a second coming of an American brewing tradition that's as old as American traditions get. Let's dust off a philosophy practically unread since Jefferson: Brewing belongs in the home, with a kettle in every kitchen, where real American beer was born.

◀ Quality
over Quantity

Craft brewing seems popular, but old drinking habits die hard. Of the almost 200 million barrels of beer produced in the U.S. in 2009, only 4.3 percent were made in craft breweries. Homebrewers made just 175,000 barrels. Still, there's hope: While overall beer sales have taken a hit during the recession, craft and homebrewed beer production is still growing.

KEN GROSSMAN

FOUNDER, SIERRA NEVADA BREWING CO.

You started homebrewing in the late '60s, before it was even legal.

I grew up down the street from a pretty accomplished homebrewer, so I was drinking home-brew before I even knew about Anchor or the other small breweries. The Maltose Falcons homebrew club was starting up in L.A. And there were a couple really eye-opening books early on about all-grain brewing and lager styles. But most homebrewing was done to save money, or make beer with a lot of alcohol.

Your friend Jack McAuliffe started New Albion in 1976, but it closed in 1983. Was that scary to see when you were starting out?

It wasn't just New Albion that was struggling. There were half a dozen small breweries failing in the late '70s. We were trying to steer clear. Everyone was operating on a shoestring budget in an untested market, which forced people to put out beer that wasn't ready. So we focused on consistency. We dumped batch after batch of pale ale before we got it to a place we knew we could replicate and be happy with. As Jack told me, the brewery is a strict mistress.

Why did you start with a pale ale, and why do you use Cascade hops?

As a homebrewer, I could brew a whole range of beers—lagers, everything. But at the brewery, we didn't have that level of technology. No lagering, no filtering. We decided that what we could do well was a bottle-conditioned ale. And we didn't want to copy an English pale and use Fuggle hops. I ran a homebrew shop, and I was buying hops from all over, and Cascades were the obvious choice. Well, back then, there wasn't a lot else being grown here.

But now you grow your own, and you even have your own rail spur to bring in barley from Canada.

That's to save energy. But yeah, as we grew, we could do more. When we expanded to our new brewery in '88, we made our first lager. We made a wet-hopped beer 14 years ago, flew in hops from Washington; it seemed like fun. We make a lot of beers that aren't widely distributed until we get the demand to package them. Demands change, people become aware of new styles. We still view ourselves as a small brewery, and we're just spreading the knowledge around. It helps the whole industry.

CHICO, CALIFORNIA

EST. 1980

SIZE: 780,000 barrels/year

OUR FAVORITES: Pale Ale, Celebration Ale, Bigfoot, Harvest Ale series

If your first beer worth remembering came in a stubby bottle, if hops have their own space on your food pyramid, if you live 1,000 miles away but know where Chico is, chances are you owe a pint to Sierra Nevada. Ken Grossman's brewery, founded in 1980 with Paul Camusi, defines craft beer. It took them weeks of failed batches, but once they nailed their flagship Pale Ale, they never changed it. Today it's so common in beer fans' top-10 lists that other brewers use the same iconic squat bottles just to get recognized as part of the scene. But Sierra Nevada's influence goes beyond that one beer. Fritz Maytag bought the first Anchor brewery 15 years earlier, but Grossman proved to a generation of beer nerds that they could start from scratch and change brewing history.

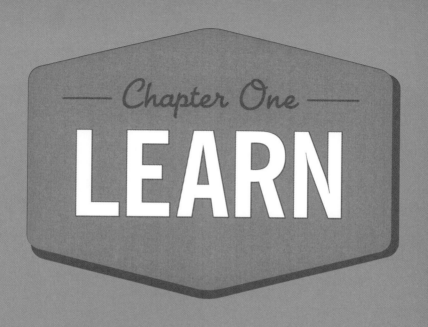

— Chapter One —
LEARN

BREWING STEPS AND **INGREDIENTS**

WHAT'S IN YOUR GLASS

Beer has only four ingredients—which means it's easy to make, and easy to make it your own. Just by changing the types of those ingredients, and their ratio, you can brew pretty much every beer style there's a name for—and even some there isn't. Beyond these basic components, everything about beer is up for grabs, so have fun!

YOUR
BEER

WATER
MALT
HOPS
YEAST

Water and grain, mixed with some sort of spice, and fermented by yeast: That's all beer is. Of course, the choice of grains, spices (hops, mostly), yeast, and, yes, even water, make all the difference—but we'll get to that later. First, let's go over the basic beer-making process.

Yeast turns sugars into alcohol, and in beer, those sugars come from barley. Brewers steep barley in hot water to make a sort of sweet, grainy tea called wort (pronounced "wert"). Different kinds of barley make the wort darker or lighter, sweeter or toastier. Brewers will then boil the wort and balance some of its sweetness by adding bitter, aromatic spices—almost always hops, though in the past, brewers used dozens more, and you can too. Hops need to be boiled to release their flavors.

Once the hopped wort cools down and brewers add yeast to it, their job is basically done. The yeast takes over, eating the sugars from the malted barley and producing alcohol and carbon dioxide in a process called fermentation. This can take a while, but when the yeast stops working, wort has turned into beer, ready to bottle, cap, and enjoy. In this chapter, we'll go over those steps in more detail, then talk about the different kinds of ingredients you can use, and how to combine them to make great-tasting homebrew.

BREWING BASICS

Clear off the kitchen stove and follow these six basic steps to your first batch of homemade beer. The following pages will go over each step in more detail, and there's a full equipment list on page 160. Consider this an overview, and a handy reference to flip back to when things get a little more complicated. Get to know this simple process, and you'll be bottling our recipes—or inventing your own—in no time.

1 MASH

Beer starts as a sugary, grain-flavored tea called wort. Make your wort by filling a mesh bag with malted grains and steeping it in hot water for an hour. You're converting starches in the grains into fermentable sugars that yeast will be able to digest into alcohol. This is called mashing.

2 SPARGE

Sparging, or rinsing your grains with hot water, extracts every last drop of sugary wort. Lift your grain bag out of the stockpot, let it drain, and dunk it in a second pot of hot water to rinse it. Then mix this water in with your wort.

3 BOIL

Hops balance wort's malty sweetness. The longer they're boiled in wort, the more bitter they'll make the beer. Typically, you'll add hops three times during an hour-long boil, for bitterness, flavor, and aroma.

4 CHILL

Chill your wort down to room temperature to make it a safe new home for yeast. Most beer yeasts will quit working—or even die—above 80°F and will hibernate below 60°F. **Make sure everything that touches your beer from this point forward is sanitized!**

5 FERMENT

It's time to put your yeast to work. Strain the chilled wort into your fermenter. Add your yeast and plug the fermenter with the stopper and tube, submerging the other end of the tube in a bowl of sanitizer. This will catch foam that will spew out when the yeast starts working. After a day, replace the tube with an airlock and wait.

6 BOTTLE

Yeast creates carbon dioxide as well as alcohol, and will naturally pressurize your bottles. Siphon your beer into a stockpot, leaving any sediment behind, and mix in a corn sugar solution. Siphon the sugared beer into bottles, cap them, and let them sit for 1 week. Then label, refrigerate, and enjoy!

CLEAN AND

SANITIZE

FIRST THING

INGREDIENTS
Water
Sanitizer

EQUIPMENT
Large bucket or tub
Spray bottle

This is the most important part of making great beer. You can fudge the other steps, but whatever you do, don't skip this one. Seriously! No matter how vigorously you scrub those countertops, your kitchen is crawling with food-loving bacteria. Your kitchen is also your brewery, and unluckily for you, there are few things those bacteria crave more than jumping into a warm bath of sugary wort. When brewing, you want your yeast to work alone.

After your beer has been boiled, keep it safe by SANITIZING EVERYTHING IT TOUCHES. Sanitizing before then is overkill—even to us—since boiling will kill anything that managed to survive up to that point. This means that your strainer, funnel, fermenter, airlock, tubing, and—when it's time—bottles and caps, should be clean and sanitary.

By SANITARY, we don't mean sterile—you're a brewer, not a chemist—so you can get what you need to treat your equipment at any homebrew shop or drugstore. Mix up a bucketful of solution (see chart at right) and soak everything in it. It helps to have a spray bottle of solution on hand, just in case anything needs a last-minute spritz.

Star-San, an acid blend, is probably the easiest sanitizer to use, since you don't need to rinse it off. Professional brewers use iodine because it's cheap to buy in bulk, but plain old bleach works, too, as long as you rinse well.

WHAT TO SANITIZE

CHILL STEP

Stockpot lid, thermometer, strainer, metal spoon, funnel, fermenter

FERMENT STEP

Blow-off tube, rubber stopper, airlock, turkey baster, hydrometer and tube

BOTTLE STEP

Bottling pot, tubing, racking cane, bottles, caps

A HOMEBREWER'S BEST FRIEND

The two most annoying things about homebrewing are peeling labels off of old bottles to reuse as your own, and cleaning out dead yeast gunk from your fermenter. Not so with Oxy-Clean. Fill a big bucket, your sink, or even a bathtub, with hot water and add a scoop. Soak your bottles for 15 minutes and their labels will slide right off. Dunk a fermenter in the bucket, and use a stiff nylon brush, or a bent toothbrush, to clean the hard-to-reach curve just below its neck.

TYPE	BRAND NAMES	AMT. PER GAL. WATER	CONTACT	RINSE
Acid	Star-San, Sani-Clean	1 tsp	30 sec	NO
Iodine	Iodophor, IO-Star	½ tsp	1 min	NO
Chlorine	Clorox bleach	1 tbsp	20 min	YES

① MASH

INGREDIENTS

Grains
Water

EQUIPMENT

Stockpot, at least 3-gallon
Stockpot, at least 2-gallon,
 with lid
Fine-mesh grain bag
Kitchen scale*
Measuring cup
Wooden spoon
Thermometer
Timer

SEE ALSO

Water, page 48
Malt, page 50
Equipment, page 160

*If you don't own a kitchen
 scale, you can measure
 your grains by volume.
 See *Grains by Volume*,
 inside front cover.

MASHING grains in hot water turns their inedible starches into a sugary banquet for beer yeast. How much grain and water you'll use, and how hot you'll steep, are determined by what beer you're making and by the behavior of enzymes in the malt. But in essence, mashing is as simple as making tea.

Start with the water. Pour 2 quarts water per pound of grain into the smaller of your two stockpots. Heat the water in your mash pot to 163°F (or the temperature specified by your recipe), then turn off the burner. This is called STRIKE WATER.

Weigh out your grains, pour them into a mesh GRAIN BAG, and sink it in the strike water. (The mesh bag will make it easy to strain out the grains later.) Fit the mouth of the bag around the lip of the pot, so it stays open but doesn't fall in, and stir the grains until they're thoroughly soaked and submerged, breaking up any dough balls that form.

Grain bag

Mash pot

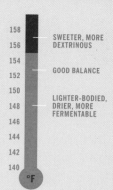

158
156 — SWEETER, MORE DEXTRINOUS
154
152 — GOOD BALANCE
150
148 — LIGHTER-BODIED, DRIER, MORE FERMENTABLE
146
144
142
140
°F

The MASH temperature should drop about 10°F once you stir in all the grains. A mash temperature of 153°F is ideal, but some beer styles benefit from mashing hotter (up to 158°F) or cooler (down to 140°F). (See HEAT AND ENZYMES, at right.)

Now put a lid on the mash and wait. You'll hold this temperature for about 1 hour to give the enzymes time to work. (Some kinds of malts, called under-modified malts, have slower-moving enzymes, and these take a bit longer to mash. Most malts you'll find these days are fast-acting and well modified, so don't worry.)

Making a DOUBLE BOILER is a perfect way to keep a steady mash temperature—just float the covered mash pot inside a larger stockpot filled with an insulating layer of 153°F water (or whatever temperature you want your mash to be). If you don't have a second stockpot big enough, you can mash in just one stockpot. Keep a closer eye on the mash temperature and turn on the burner when needed.

Check the temperature of the mash every 15 minutes, and record it in your brew log (see page 164). After an hour, it's time to sparge.

HEAT AND ENZYMES

Enzymes are the machines that turn starches into sugars in a process called saccharification. Different enzymes work best at different temperatures, and produce different-tasting beers. Alpha-amylase, for example, converts long-chain starches into sugar molecules called dextrins. Beer yeast can't ferment dextrins, so they remain in the finished beer, making it rich and sweet. Alpha-amylase likes a warmer mash. Beta-amylase, on the other hand, operates at cooler temperatures, and converts starches into easily fermentable sugars like maltose, which makes for a crisper, drier beer. Adjusting your mash temperature will affect your final beer, but only to a point. Enzyme activity shuts down below 140°F and above 158°F, so always keep your mash between those bookends.

② SPARGE

INGREDIENTS
Mashed grains
Water

EQUIPMENT
Stockpot, at least 3-gallon
Stockpot, at least 2-gallon
Fine-mesh grain bag
Measuring cup
Thermometer

SEE ALSO
Equipment, page 160

When your mash is finished, it's time to collect your **WORT**. This is what brewers call the sweet grain tea—a kind of proto-beer—that remains after you remove your spent grains. Since all your grain is in a mesh bag, this is as easy as lifting the grain bag out of the mash pot and letting the wort drain back in. Be patient and don't squeeze, or you'll extract bitter tannins from the grain husks. (If your pot has a pasta insert, you can rest your grain bag inside it for about 5 minutes to drain.)

On average, grains in a mash soak up ½ quart of water per pound, so if you mashed 3 pounds of grain in 6 quarts of water, you'll drain off about 4½ quarts of wort. This wort is called the **FIRST RUNNINGS**. It's super sugary and very dark.

If you grab a few grains out of the drained bag and chew them, you'll notice they're still a little sweet. You want to get every bit of sugar out of the grains and into your beer to give your

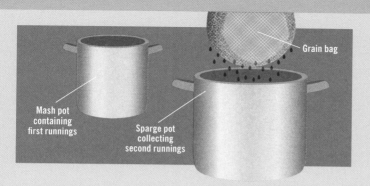

Grain bag

Mash pot containing first runnings

Sparge pot collecting second runnings

yeast as much food as possible, so after you drain the first runnings, you'll rinse the grains in SPARGE WATER.

SPARGE means "to sprinkle," and in professional breweries and large-scale homebrew setups, that's literally what happens—a hose sprays warm water over the mashed grains; the water trickles through and is collected as wort.

All you need to do, though, is dunk your grain bag in a pot of fresh hot water for a few minutes, then mix those SECOND RUNNINGS in with the first. If you mashed in a double boiler, just use your big insulating pot. You'll have to add more water to it, though.

You need to collect 2 gallons (8 quarts) of wort total before you boil because in an hour of boiling about a gallon of wort will evaporate. So measure your first runnings, then use enough sparge water to bring the total volume up to 2 gallons.

Add the sparge water to a second stockpot and heat it to 165°F. (Be careful not to go hotter, or you'll leach out astringent tannins.) Sink your grain bag, slosh it around a bit, but try not to squeeze. Let it soak for 15 minutes, then drain as before. Combine this water with the first runnings in the smaller of your two stockpots, and you're ready to boil.

SPARGING BIGGER BEERS

The amount of wort you'll collect from your first and second runnings—and what you'll do with it—changes slightly if you're brewing bigger beers. Barleywines and strong abbey beers need to be boiled longer than the usual hour (up to 90 minutes or more). This concentrates the wort, making the final beer stronger, and the more intense heat caramelizes some of the sugars, adding complexity. Some breweries will make a strong beer from the first runnings alone, and a weaker "small beer" from the second runnings. But in 1-gallon batches, it's easier to stick with a longer boil. Because more wort will evaporate during a longer boil, you'll need to collect more wort to begin with—2½ gallons, at least—so use more sparge water.

③ BOIL

INGREDIENTS

Wort
Hops

EQUIPMENT

Stockpot, at least 2-gallon, with lid
Gram scale*
Timer
Large metal spoon

SEE ALSO

Hops, page 58
Equipment, page 160

*If you don't own a gram scale, you can measure your hops by area. See *Hops by Area*, inside front cover.

You should now have a stockpot filled with 2 gallons of wort. This will serve as your BREW KETTLE. (If your brew kettle is filled to the brim, you might want to start your boil in the larger stockpot—then transfer it to the smaller one after about 30 minutes—to avoid a boil-over.)

Turn on the heat and bring the wort to a vigorous boil. BOILING your wort sanitizes it, concentrates its sugars, smooths out its body by coagulating proteins from the grains, and lets you flavor your beer with hops or other spices, since the heat extracts their bitter acids and aromatic oils.

On average, the boil will take 1 hour and you'll add hops at three different points.

As your wort comes to a boil, you'll notice a thick brown foam roll over it. These are proteins. When the foam starts clumping together and sinking back into the pot you've reached the HOT BREAK. This usually happens

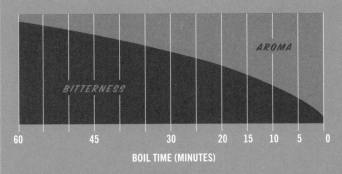

HOP BITTERNESS AND AROMA OVER TIME

AROMA

BITTERNESS

60   45   30   20   15   10   5   0

BOIL TIME (MINUTES)

The bittering acids in hops intensify the longer they're boiled, while the aromatic oils weaken. This means that powerful hops work best when added early and subtler hops should be boiled less. You can also add complex levels of flavor and aroma to your beer by mixing the hop styles you use in the middle of a boil, since they'll contribute acids as well as oils.

right when the wort starts to boil, but may take longer. Getting those proteins to fall out of suspension with a vigorous boil and a good hot break will make your beer clearer and cleaner tasting.

Make sure to watch your brew kettle closely, and never put a lid on it. BOIL-OVERS can come out of nowhere, turning your stove into a sticky mess.

Once the wort boils, it's time to add hops. The longer hops are boiled, the more bitter they get, so this first addition is called the BITTERING ADDITION. The amount and variety of hops you'll use varies from recipe to recipe. Just toss in the hops and stir them around

a bit to help them dissolve. You'll usually add hops two more times: about 40 minutes into the boil, for the last 20 minutes (the FLAVORING HOPS); and 60 minutes in, right before you turn off the heat (for AROMA).

After you finish your boil, stir the wort into a WHIRLPOOL with a sanitized metal spoon. Stir clockwise for at least 30 seconds to get things going. This helps floating bits of hops and grain settle to the bottom of the pot and keeps them from getting into your finished beer.

Now put a sanitized lid on your stockpot, and start chilling your wort.

④ CHILL

INGREDIENTS

Hot wort
Ice (5 trays or a 5-lb bag)
Cold water

EQUIPMENT

Stockpot, at least 3-gallon
Stockpot, at least 2-gallon,
 with lid
Thermometer
Strainer
Funnel
Fermenter
Sanitizer

SEE ALSO

Clean and Sanitize, page 30
Equipment, page 160

Once you stop boiling, everything that touches your wort must be SANITIZED! We mean it! Even with a lid on, your pot of boiled wort is prime real estate for bacteria, so you want to get it sealed in a fermenter as soon as you can. The problem is, wort this hot will kill yeast, so you need to chill it first.

Fill your larger stockpot about halfway with ice and cold water, and float your covered brew kettle inside it. Add fresh ice as the water between the pots heats up and the ice melts. If you don't have a larger stockpot, chill in your sink—it works, but it'll take longer.

If you take a peek under the lid, you'll see light-brown clumps of protein sinking to the bottom of the pot. This is the COLD BREAK. Just like with the hot break, the faster you go, the more protein will settle out and the smoother your beer will be. Proteins left in suspension when the wort goes into the fermenter can cause what's called "chill haze" and cloud your beer when you put it in the fridge. Yeah, it's only cosmetic, but why not make beer that looks as good as it tastes?

Chill your wort to 70°F or cooler. It should take about 30 minutes. Don't stir the wort or slosh it around as it chills—you want the cold break material and any grain or hop particles to settle out cleanly, falling to the bottom of the pot. This layer of sediment is called TRUB. It's bitter, gritty, and all around pretty gross. Keep as much of it as possible out of your beer.

When the wort is cool enough, carefully pour it through a sanitized, fine-mesh metal strainer (we use a gold coffee filter) and funnel it into your sanitized fermenter, leaving the trub behind. If your strainer gets clogged with trub, just rinse it out.

You should end up with 1 gallon of wort in your fermenter. (About 1 quart will be lost to trub.) A little more or less isn't a problem. (If you end up with much less than a gallon, top off your fermenter with tap water. It'll make for a weaker, watery beer, but it's better than over-carbonated—and potentially explosive—bottles. Trust us!)

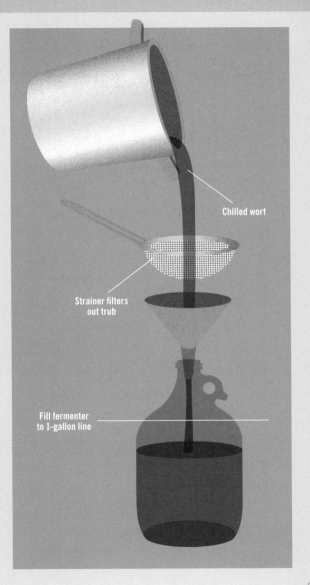

Chilled wort

Strainer filters out trub

Fill fermenter to 1-gallon line

⑤ FERMENT

INGREDIENTS
Chilled wort
Yeast

EQUIPMENT
Fermenter
Blow-off tube
  (1⅛" in diameter)
Mason jar
Rubber stopper
Airlock
Hydrometer with tube
Turkey baster

SEE ALSO
Clean and Sanitize, page 30
Yeast, page 64
Equipment, page 160

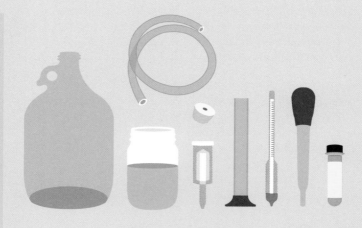

Before you add the yeast, take a HYDROMETER reading and record it in your brew log. This is your beer's ORIGINAL GRAVITY. (See USING A HYDROMETER, at right.) If the hydrometer and tube are sanitized, you can pour the sample back into the fermenter when you're done—but save a little to taste. It should be sweet and bitter—a good sign of great beer to come.

Now it's time to pour in—or PITCH—your yeast. How much you need to add depends on how sugary your wort is.

The more sugars, the more yeast is needed to ferment them into alcohol and turn your wort into beer. In general, you'll use about ¼ tube of liquid yeast per batch. Make sure the yeast is at room temperature, and add it to your fermenter.

Yeast ferments anaerobically—that is, without oxygen—but it begins life breathing air. To make sure it gets a healthy start, shake up the fermenter for a full minute to AERATE the wort (being careful not to spill). We use a sanitized cappuccino foamer, stirring for about 10 seconds, to make extra sure.

Plug your fermenter with a wide vinyl tube, about 1⅛ inch in diameter. It should fit snugly inside the mouth. This is a blow-off tube. Put the other end in a small jar, half-full of sanitizer, and stash the whole thing in a cool, dark place. After about 12 hours, the yeast will gather on top of the wort in a thick layer of foam called KRAEUSEN. You'll notice some brownish gunk riding the foam—German brewers call this "braun hefe," or brown yeast, but it's actually a mix of wort proteins, hop resins, and dead yeast cells. It's bitter and gross, and many brewers skim it off and chuck it. In your case, it'll foam up through your blow-off tube and safely out of your beer. After a day or two, when the foam subsides, it's safe to replace the blow-off tube with

USING A HYDROMETER

A hydrometer measures the amount of dissolved solids in a liquid—in our case, sugars in beer. Arabian chemists were using devices like this in the 11th century, but the technology was first applied to beer by British brewer John Richardson in 1785.

To take a measurement, pour a sample of wort into a hydrometer tube and float the hydrometer in it. The higher it floats, the denser the wort and the more sugars it contains. Plain water has a gravity of 1.000. Wort can range from 1.025 (for a low-alcohol beer) to 1.150 (for an imperial).

Using a hydrometer lets you predict how alcoholic your beer will be, since the more sugary it is going into fermentation, the more sugars your yeast will eat, and the more alcohol they'll produce. If you know your beer's gravity before fermentation (its original gravity) and after fermentation (its final gravity), you can be exact. Subtract the final gravity from the original gravity and multiply by 131.25 to get the alcohol by volume (ABV). A 1.040 wort fermented to a 1.010 beer will be 3.9 percent ABV. Keep in mind that hydrometers are only accurate when your wort is 60°F—use your hydrometer's conversion chart to make adjustments at higher temperatures.

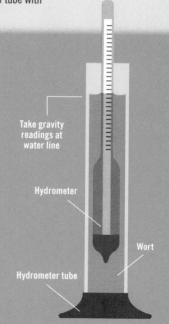

Take gravity readings at water line

Hydrometer

Wort

Hydrometer tube

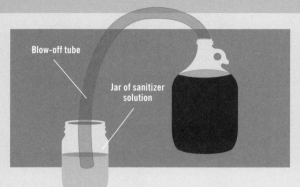

Blow-off tube

Jar of sanitizer solution

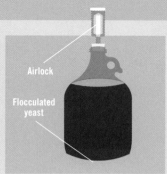

Airlock

Flocculated yeast

a sanitized AIRLOCK filled with water (see HOW TO USE AN AIRLOCK, at right).

And now, you wait. Sunlight can deteriorate hop molecules, so keep your fermenter covered. Most yeasts like to ferment at room temperature, or a tad cooler, but the yeasts that make lager beers need special care (see LEARN TO LAGER, at right). Use a sanitized turkey baster to take hydrometer measurements every few days to check your beer's progress. As it ferments and sugars turn into less-dense alcohol, the hydrometer reading will fall. Other than that, leave your beer alone!

If your beer is bubbling, you know it's fermenting. This active, PRIMARY FERMENTATION can take just a few days for an average ale, but can take up to a few weeks for very strong beers, or cold-fermented lagers. When the bubbles in the airlock subside and the yeast

FLOCCULATES, or falls to the bottom of your fermenter, primary fermentation is over. At this point, you might siphon your beer off that sediment into a clean, SECONDARY FERMENTER for long-term aging. (Beer left on top of yeast sediment for too long—a month or more—will pick up some off flavors from the dead cells.) But only a few styles of beer—like barleywine and lagers—need to be conditioned this long.

Most beer is ready to bottle about a week after primary fermentation finishes. This gives the beer a little extra time to clear, and lets the remaining active yeast cells clean up any of their messy by-products. In other words, when the gravity stops dropping, the yeast has flocculated, the beer has cleared, and—most importantly—it tastes good enough to drink. For most styles, this whole process takes about 10 days. Then you're ready to bottle!

HOW TO USE AN AIRLOCK

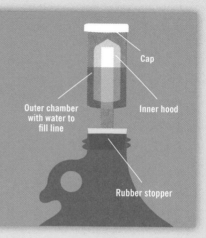

Airlocks let carbon dioxide bubble out of the fermenter, but keep any bacteria-laden air from getting in. We use water to fill airlocks, just in case a little drips into the fermenting beer. (Sanitizer would kill the yeast.) If you're using a one-piece, S-shaped airlock, add enough water to fill each bubble halfway.

If you're using a three-piece airlock, like we do, fill the outside chamber with water up to the fill line, plug your fermenter with the rubber stopper, fit in the airlock, then drop in the inner plastic hood and cap it. The inner hood should float, suspended in water. During fermentation, as bubbles come up out of the fermenter, the inner hood will gently rise and fall along with them.

LEARN TO LAGER

Lager yeasts are finicky beasts. If the temperature isn't cool enough for them, they'll throw off all sorts of nasty flavors. If you're after the crisp, clean lager taste of pilsners or bocks, you'll need to ferment your beer at 55°F or cooler (see PILSNER recipe, page 94).

Keep your fermenter in a cold basement, or—even better—in a souped-up mini fridge (see page 162). After about 1 week, when primary fermentation finishes and the beer begins to clear, it's time to lager, or cold-condition. Take your fermenter out of the basement or fridge, and let it come back to room temperature for a day. This is called a diacetyl rest, and gives the yeast an energy boost to scrub out any extra bad flavors floating around, before things get quiet. Now siphon your beer into a second, clean and sanitized, fermenter, and put it back in the fridge or basement. Try to keep this fermenter even colder: 45°F for a full month, but cooler and longer is better. This helps the yeast settle out and makes for a much clearer, cleaner beer.

6 BOTTLE

INGREDIENTS

Beer!
Water
Corn sugar

EQUIPMENT

Hydrometer and tube
Stockpot
Turkey baster
Bottle capper*
10 brown glass bottles
10 bottle caps
Tubing (⅛" in diameter)
Small racking cane
Hose clamp or binder clip
Small bowl
Sanitizer

SEE ALSO

Clean and Sanitize, page 30
Design, page 137
Equipment, page 160

*Or you can buy half a
dozen swing-top Grolsch
16-ouncers and bottle
your beer in them.

It's time! Your beer has finished fermenting, you've collected 10 or so empties (the best part of homebrewing), and you're ready to bottle. Most breweries force-carbonate their bottles by mixing beer with carbon dioxide as they package it; you'll be carbonating your beer naturally, by letting the few remaining active yeast cells pressurize the bottles. (Yes, there are still some live ones floating around, even if you can't see them.) All you need to do is give them a bit more food, called PRIMING SUGAR.

First, take a FINAL GRAVITY reading. Use a sanitized turkey baster to pull a sample from your fermenter. It should be somewhere around 1.010, depending on which yeast strain you used. Some "highly attenuating" strains eat more sugars and make for a drier and less dense beer than others. Have a taste. Delicious? Of course it is.

Sanitize a stockpot and pour in 1 cup of water. Boil it with 1 ounce of corn sugar for 1 minute to dissolve and sanitize the sugar. (Some recipes call for different kinds of priming sugar, but corn sugar is tasteless, and therefore most widely used. You can substitute cane sugar if that's all you have on hand.) Let the sugar solution cool down to room temperature before you transfer your beer into the pot.

Now you'll move your finished beer from the fermenter to the pot. The goal is to leave as much sediment behind in your fermenter has possible, so you'll use a racking cane and tubing to siphon off the liquid. (Remember, all your equipment must be SANITIZED—that means all your tubing, your racking cane, and especially all your bottles and caps.)

Siphoning happens quickly, so arrange your filling station before you get started. Place your fermenter on a high counter, and your bottling pot on the floor below. Put any old bowl next to the bottling pot to catch siphoning runoff. Let your bottles and caps soak in a bucket of sanitizer while you complete this first step.

Attach a long tube fitted with a hose clamp to the short end of your racking cane. Stick the long end of the cane into your sanitizer bucket, and suck through the tube to fill the whole contraption with sanitizer. Close the hose

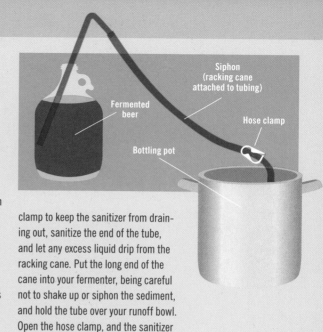

Siphon (racking cane attached to tubing)

Fermented beer

Hose clamp

Bottling pot

clamp to keep the sanitizer from draining out, sanitize the end of the tube, and let any excess liquid drip from the racking cane. Put the long end of the cane into your fermenter, being careful not to shake up or siphon the sediment, and hold the tube over your runoff bowl. Open the hose clamp, and the sanitizer in the tube should pour out, followed quickly by your beer. Switch from the runoff bowl to the bottling pot and fill.

Move your bottling pot to the countertop, drain your bottles, and arrange them on the floor next to the runoff bowl. Set up a new siphon and, using the hose clamp to stop and start the flow, fill each bottle to 1 inch from the top.

Cap the bottles, and let them carbonate in a dark corner for 1 to 2 weeks. Then label (see page 144), and stash them in the fridge.

CHILL TIME

Once your bottles are carbonated and safely stored in the fridge, it helps to let them sit for a little while longer. Lighter beers like wheat beers and pale ales are ready to drink quickly, but darker stuff like stouts and Scottish ales might taste too sharp and roasty at first. A week of cold storage helps blend those flavors. For some beers, a month or two is even better. So be patient—if you can.

BRET AND ERIC KUHNHENN

FOUNDERS, KUHNHENN BREWING COMPANY

Tell us about your equipment.

BRET: We were brewing 12-gallon batches at home, and then we found a 90-gallon coffee maker on eBay for $100. I guess they use them in prisons or the Army. Today we boil in an eight-barrel "brew-on-premises" [BOP] system, also from eBay, and a kettle that used to be a sourdough yeast starter for a bread company. Our hot liquor tank [a big tub that heats water for mashing and sparging] was a peanut butter tank from Quaker Oats.

The BOP system is for customers to make small batches of their own beers, but it also means you guys can work on multiple recipes at once.

BRET: Yeah, we'll do experimental stuff like brewing 13 different wheat beers. We'll have a party and try them all and then put one into rotation. But usually, every beer we make is totally different. We'll change the mash program, change the yeast every time. It's just like homebrew!

Are there drawbacks to brewing on such a small system?

BRET: We usually make the beer very concentrated, ferment it out, then add water to cut it because we don't have enough space to make undiluted batches. All the big guys like Miller do that, but they add water in-line.

And they add way more water than you do.

BRET: We're known for big beers. That's just what we love. And we hope people buy it. For some beers, though, we have to have a one-per-visit rule, just so people know it's strong. Plus, we usually don't have a lot of it.

It seems like you guys have brewed pretty much everything. Are there any beers you don't make?

ERIC: We were one of the first breweries to age beer in wine barrels. We aged a Belgian strong ale in a Syrah barrel—and we made the wine, too. Do you know Westvleteren 12? [One of the most famous beers on earth, and impossible to find outside the Trappist monastery that brews it.] We're working on something like that. Or maybe something better.

BRET: But we don't make a lot of brown ales. I don't like 'em.

WARREN, MICHIGAN
EST. 1998
SIZE: 800 barrels/year
OUR FAVORITES: Cherry Oud Bruin, Crème Brûlée Java Stout, Mittlefruh Monster, Extraneous, Mayhem, and all the meads

Bret and Eric Kuhnhenn were just a couple of homebrewing kids in suburban Detroit, till one day in 1996, they convinced their dad to start selling brewing gear in his hardware store. With ingredients at their fingertips (and at wholesale prices), they went wild, scraping together bigger and bigger systems until their brewery eclipsed the hardware store. It's a homebrewer-made-good kind of story: They're still messing around with small, experimental batches, only these days they brew for a barful of thirsty regulars and under a ceiling dripping with gold medals won around the world and brought home to Warren. The brothers make mead, wine, and some of the most intense beers we've ever had, loaded with cherries or coffee or compressed into a portlike bomb of booze and flavor. Oh, and they still sell homebrew kits across the street.

WATER

PRICE

Cost of water is negligible, though relative to other ingredients, you'll be using a lot of it. Additives used for water treatment—like gypsum and calcium carbonate—run only a few pennies per batch.

USAGE

It takes about 6 gallons of water to homebrew a typical small batch. You'll use about 3 gallons for mashing and sparging, 2 for sanitizing, and 1 (in the form of ice) for chilling.

SEE ALSO

Mash, page 32

You probably don't pay much attention to what comes out of your faucet, but in beer, everything matters—even the water. In fact, some of the world's most popular beer styles, such as pale ales and pilsners, owe their character to the water first used to brew them.

What your water is like determines what your beer is like because certain minerals get along better than others with the enzymes in a mash and with the chemistry of hops and yeast. Generally, if your water tastes fine from the faucet, it's fine to brew with. But understanding some basic chemistry can't hurt. It might even help you identify some off flavors down the road.

TYPES OF WATER

Water is hard or soft, and acidic or alkaline, depending on the types and amounts of minerals and ions dissolved in it. We'll start with pH. This measures how acidic a liquid is, based on how many ionized water molecules are in it. The enzymes at work in a mash like their water acidity to be on the high side, which, to keep things confusing, corresponds to a lower pH number. A quick swipe through your mash with a pH test strip will let you know if you're in the ballpark, say, around 5.1 to 5.4.

HARD WATER Some minerals are good. Calcium, for instance, reduces tannins in wort; sodium helps make beer fuller and sweeter; and a touch of magnesium is good for the health of your yeast. Too much of anything, though (especially carbonate and bicarbonate, which make beer darker and more astringent), becomes instantly noticeable in a beer. That's not always a bad thing: The sulfate-rich water in England's Burton-on-Trent amplified hop bitterness, giving birth to the iconic pale ale.

SOFT WATER Generally speaking, soft water is better than hard water for brewing, because minerals are easier to add than to take out. The fewer minerals, the cleaner tasting your beer will be—up to a point, of course. The water in Pilsen in the Czech Republic is useless for brewing anything but crystal-clear Pilsners. Its water is naturally so empty of minerals that it's hard for yeast to live in it, forcing brewers to use complicated mashing techniques to produce a wort healthy enough to make beer.

Easy Treat

Most cities add some amount of chlorine to their water supply. If you can taste it, there's too much, and it might make your beer taste harsh. The fix is as easy as running your mash water through a Brita, or any charcoal filter.

PRACTICAL ADVICE

STICK WITH THE TAP It's probably fine, and might even lead to some unique brews. Even if it smells like rotten eggs—just think of the brewers in Burton-on-Trent, and make do. Brewing with bottled water is too expensive to be any fun, and using too much mineral-poor distilled water will create yeast-health problems more trouble than they're worth.

BASIC ADJUSTMENTS Check your mash pH to get a quick sense of how hard or soft your water is. Buy a tube of pH papers at your homebrew store, or make a call to your water department.

PROBLEM	TREATMENT
Too soft?	Add ¼ tsp of gypsum per gallon of mash water
Too hard?	Brew darker beers (dark, acidic malts balance mineral-rich water) or dilute with a few cups of distilled water per gallon of mash water
Too acidic?	Add ¼ tsp of calcium carbonate per gallon of mash water
Too basic?	Add ¼ tsp of gypsum or calcium chloride per gallon of mash water

MALT

PRICE

$1 to $2 per pound

USAGE

2 to 4 pounds per gallon-
size batch (less for session
beers, more for the strongest imperials)

STORAGE

6 months or more if they're
kept dry

SEE ALSO

Mash, page 32
Specialty Grains, page 100

Beer is barley. The color of your beer, how rich and sweet it is, whether it's heavy or light, and much of its aroma come from its foundation: grain.

Alcohol is made when yeast eats sugar. Change the sugar, and you change the booze you'll make—glucose and fructose from grapes will get you wine; maltose, from grains, will make beer. Theoretically, you could brew with any grain, but the beauty of barley is that it not only tastes great once fermented (unlike, say, corn, which only comes into its own after it's fermented, distilled, then aged) but that it ferments pretty easily too. All barley needs is a little coaxing from a process called malting.

Brewers can't just toss some fresh-from-the-field barley stalks into a pot to make a batch of beer. First, they need to get at the grain's hidden starches and convert them to fermentable sugars. But barley hides them well. So we trick it into growing and releasing those starches for us. Maltsters steep grains in water until they just start to sprout, sending out tiny roots called chits. At this point, the grains are called "green malt." Then, maltsters throw on the brakes, chop off the roots, and dry the seeds—producing malt proper.

While sprouting, each barley grain produces enzymes that the plant uses to unlock a piece of tissue called endosperm, open its stores of starch, and convert the starches into sugars that the plant will need to grow. But drying the grains stops the growth and leaves the starches hanging out, waiting for you—the brewer. Now the barley's ready to be steeped in hot water, which will extract those starches and convert them into sugar—maltose, to be exact. This process is called mashing, and you already know how to do that. But before you brew, you have to go shopping. Here's what to keep in mind:

CHARACTERISTICS OF GRAIN

Malted barley is categorized according to three general properties: modification, diastatic power, and degrees Lovibond. If you order your grains online, they'll probably be sorted by one or all of these.

Modification measures sugar. The more starches available in a kind of malt, the more modified the malt is. Highly modified malts like American 2-Row are full of fermentable sugars to extract in a mash, and making beer out of them is super easy. Under-modified malts, like some pilsner malts, need outside help—from other malted grains—or different mashing techniques.

Diastatic power measures enzymes. The more enzymes, the more power. Malts with very high diastatic power have so many enzymes that they can convert starches from other grains as well as from themselves. Using high-power malts—called base malts—lets you build complex, multi-grain beers. Roasting malt destroys its enzymes but adds lots of color and aroma. That's why you can't make a beer using only Black Patent malt—although it makes a great addition to a base of standard American 2-Row.

Degrees Lovibond are a measure of color. Once malt is dried, it's ready to use, but putting grains through extra processing will change the final color and flavor of your beer. Roasting malted grain is a bit like toasting bread—the grain gets darker and smells great. As simple as that seems, it's explained by one of chemistry's more complicated formulas, the Maillard reaction: Sugars heat up and combine with broken protein chains to produce melanoidins, which color the beer but don't have any flavor, and aromatic compounds, which give roasted malt its toasty smell. The higher the Lovibond number, the more toasted the grain—and the darker the resulting beer.

ENDOSPERM
ACROSPIRE
HUSK
CHITS

Inside Malted Grain

Within barley's papery husk is the starch-packed endosperm and a tiny embryo. When the grain germinates, enzymes open the endosperm, feeding the embryo, which grows roots, called chits, and a sprout, called an acrospire.

TYPES OF MALT

Based on those characteristics, brewers divide malts according to how they're used. Malts with a lot of diastatic power, for example, serve as your beer's foundation; darkly roasted malts work better as accents.

BASE MALT American 2-Row, Pale Ale, British Maris Otter, and Belgian Pilsner malt (all 2-row, of course) will form the base of almost every beer you'll make. They're packed full of enzymes and have relatively neutral flavors. These malts aren't roasted at all, and are dried at low enough temperatures to keep all their enzymes intact.

FLAVOR MALT These are the all-arounders. Flavor malts are kilned a bit hotter than base malts, which gives them a boost of roasted, nutty flavor, and a darker color, but still preserves some of their enzymes. They have just enough diastatic power that it's technically possible, though dicey, to make a beer entirely of flavor malts. They'll convert their own starches to sugars, but they aren't strong enough to work on anything else. They're a good choice for malty, dark amber beers like Oktoberfest Märzens.

ROASTED MALT These malts add color and rich, dark notes, like coffee and chocolate—or even charcoal—to your beer. They're regular barley grains that are malted and dried as usual, then roasted at high heat. The longer they're roasted, the sharper their flavor and the darker their color.

CRYSTAL MALT These are green malts that are dried quickly at very high temperatures to liquefy and caramelize the lump of starch inside each grain. This process will keep some of the malt's sugars from fermenting, so they'll add a residual sweetness to your beer, plus flavor notes that range from raisins to toffee to freshly baked bread. Crystal (or Caramel) malt is sold according to its color (measured in degrees Lovibond), which indicates how dark and richly sweet each variety is— from light (20°L) to very dark (120°L).

2-ROW BARLEY   6-ROW BARLEY

What Is 2-Row Malt?

Six-row barley has six rows of seeds on a stalk; 2-row has two. Six-row barley is much easier to farm than 2-row—fields can produce about twice as much of it per acre—so naturally, it's the main type of barley that Americans grow, and it's cheap. The problem is, 6-row barley has more protein than 2-row, making for thicker, oilier beers, not Miller Lite. So big American breweries thin out their 6-row malt with low-protein grains like corn and rice. They've been doing it since the 19th century, even before corn and rice became the cheap, throwaway adjuncts they are today. Craft brewers and home-brewers stick to 2-row malt. It's a bit pricier, but it tastes great and there's no need to water it down.

SPECIALTY GRAINS AND ADJUNCTS Barley's best, but why stop there? Other grains—like rye, wheat, oats, and even rice—can add new dimensions to a regular, all-barley brew. Besides having their own unique flavors, a lot of these grains are full of proteins that can give your beer extra body, like a shot of steroids. Some specialty grains will come malted and can be tossed right into a mash; others—known as adjuncts—require a special mashing technique (see page 101).

PRACTICAL ADVICE

CHOOSING GRAINS AND PREDICTING FLAVOR Each batch of beer you make will use about two pounds of base malt, and up to one pound of flavor, crystal, and/or roasted malts. Your local homebrew shop will have barrels full of the stuff, and choosing can be overwhelming. Don't worry! Open a couple bins and stick your nose in. Is the aroma strong or subtle? Smoky? Sweet? Chocolatey? Pop a few grains in your mouth. Are they harsh and brittle? Soft and toasty? Besides tap water, of course, grains are the only major ingredient in beer you can easily sample raw, so go wild.

MILLING YOUR GRAIN The idea with milling, or crushing, malts is to break open their husks without pulverizing them. That way, hot mash water can get at the endosperm inside the grains, while their papery shells help keep the mash porous when you strain it. Homebrew shops will crush grain for you, usually for free. You can buy your own mill if you want—they're expensive ($50-100), but worlds better for your beer than going at the kernels with a rolling pin—or worse, a coffee grinder.

STOCKING UP Buy in bulk. Grain is easy to store as long as you remember: Moisture is the enemy. There's no real need to keep grains in your fridge, unless the air is quite hot and humid. Just keep them out of sunlight and away from heat, and double-ziplock them. They'll keep for months, if you're careful. After more than a year, especially if it gets very hot, grain can go rancid—but that's a rare concern.

What Is Extract?

Syrupy malt extracts are made by steeping malted grains in hot water to make wort, then evaporating most of the water in a vacuum (or all of the water, in the case of powdered extracts). The extra processing compromises the flavor a bit, and it's expensive, so extracts are available for only a few types of malt—"light," "dark," and "amber" among them.

FIELD GUIDE TO GRAINS

This is your field guide to the world of grain. These 30 varieties are the basics, but you might come across others, or see these same grains under different names. That's because some maltsters trademark their particular roasts. The American maltster Breiss calls its Biscuit malt "Victory." And Weyermann's German, aromatic malt is called "Melanoidin." You can also find organic and pesticide-free versions of some of these, but they, too, might have a different name. Find something not on the chart? Experiment! Chew a few grains to test the flavor out, or better yet, try it in a beer. We've included average Lovibond (color) ratings, and weight guidelines for a basic recipe.

BELGIAN PILSNER MALT
2°L

Super light and smooth. The base for almost all lagers, dark or light.

AMERICAN 2-ROW MALT
2°L

Packed with enzymes. A great base if you're using lots of other malts.

WHEAT MALT
3°L

Has only enough enzymes to make up, at most, ⅔ of the base malts in your mash.

PALE ALE MALT
3°L

A bit toastier than other base malts, but with slightly less diastatic power.

MARIS OTTER MALT
4°L

Deep, nutty, and complex—the Rolls-Royce of base malts. Shines on its own.

2–4 LBS BASE MALTS

VIENNA MALT
4°L

Light, sweet, with a slight aroma of caramel. Good addition to pilsners.

MUNICH MALT
8°L

Malty and toasty aroma, reddish in color.

AROMATIC MALT
20°L

Basically a darker Munich. Has a very rich aroma (duh).

HONEY MALT
25°L

Tastes and smells like honey on a biscuit.

BISCUIT MALT
27°L

Light aroma but warm, toasty flavor. Good for Abbey ales, browns, and porters.

5–15 OZ FLAVOR MALTS

BROWN MALT
50°L

Dry and bready. Traditional brown ales and porters can be made of almost ½ Brown malt.

COFFEE MALT
150°L

Rich, complex coffee flavor.

CHOCOLATE MALT
350°L

Sweet and nutty, but can be sharply bitter, too—consider it a lighter Black Patent malt.

CARAFA MALT
425°L

Deep, dark toast. Comes de-husked for minimal tannic bite. Just a dash turns an IPA black.

BLACK PATENT MALT
550°L

Sharp burnt flavor. Darkens beer foam.

1–5 OZ ROASTED MALTS

20°L CRYSTAL
20°L

Mildly sweet, and golden in color. Adds as much body as flavor.

40°L CRYSTAL
40°L

Has a sweeter, more caramely flavor than 20°L Crystal, but is still very light. Baked-bread aroma.

60°L CRYSTAL
60°L

Stronger and warmer in flavor and aroma. Lightly toasty as well, with an amber color.

80°L CRYSTAL
80°L

Aroma and flavor of toffee or dark bread.

120°L CRYSTAL
120°L

Very rich, deep, caramelized sweetness, with notes of raisin and fig.

1–10 OZ CRYSTAL MALTS

CARAPILS MALT
2°L

Also called Dextrin malt. Adds no color or flavor, but lots of body to your beer.

CARAMUNICH MALT
45°L

Adds body and a deep, reddish color. Classic for dark lagers.

SPECIAL B MALT
145°L

A very dark Crystal malt, with complex notes of raisins and toffee. Good in darker Belgian ales.

SMOKED MALT
2°L

Smoky! Your beer will smell like bacon. Some German beers are 100% smoked malt.

RYE MALT
4°L

Crisp and spicy flavor, but gets sticky in the mash.

5–10 OZ SPECIALTY MALTS

CORN
1°L

Also sold as flaked maize. Lightens body. Grainy, umami-like flavor.

RICE
1°L

Flavor is crisp, with light fruit notes, depending on the variety. Lightens body.

OATS
1°L

Sold as flaked oats. Creates smooth, rich body, but using too much will kill your beer's foam.

WHEAT
2°L

Sold as flaked, torrified, or unmalted wheat. Good for head retention and body.

ROASTED BARLEY
550°L

Even drier and sharper than Black Patent malt, so use sparingly. Gives Guinness its bite.

5–10 OZ UNMALTED GRAINS AND ADJUNCTS

YOUR BREW

65–100% BASE MALTS
0–35% SPECIALTY MALTS
0–15% ADJUNCT GRAINS

PALE ALE

90% AMERICAN 2-ROW MALT
10% 20°L CRYSTAL MALT

BROWN ALE

78% PALE ALE MALT
8% 40°L CRYSTAL MALT
8% BROWN MALT
3% CHOCOLATE MALT
3% WHEAT MALT

WHEAT BEER

50% WHEAT MALT
50% BELGIAN PILSNER MALT

SAISON

85% BELGIAN PILSNER MALT
10% WHEAT MALT
5% VIENNA MALT

ABBEY ALE

83% BELGIAN PILSNER MALT
10% MUNICH MALT
5% SPECIAL B MALT
2% AROMATIC MALT

PORTER

70% AMERICAN 2-ROW MALT
12% 60°L CRYSTAL MALT
7% CARAMUNICH MALT
7% CHOCOLATE MALT
4% BLACK PATENT MALT

STOUT

85% MARIS OTTER MALT
10% ROASTED BARLEY
5% FLAKED WHEAT

SCOTTISH ALE

65% MARIS OTTER MALT
13% 60°L CRYSTAL MALT
7% 120°L CRYSTAL MALT
7% HONEY MALT
7% AROMATIC MALT
1% ROASTED BARLEY

PILSNER

92% BELGIAN PILSNER MALT
8% CARAPILS MALT

BARLEY-WINE

92% MARIS OTTER MALT
5% BISCUIT MALT
3% 80°L CRYSTAL MALT

SAME BEER, BUT ONLY BARLEY

Never mind the flavoring power of water, hops, and yeast—malts make the biggest mark. Change these, and you change almost everything. The malt profiles here reflect the basic recipes in this book, but they are, of course, only guidelines. Get a sense of what makes a stout a stout (or what doesn't), then break the rules.

HOPS

PRICE

$2 to $3 per ounce (which works out to about 10 cents per gram—and $1 to $3 per batch)

USAGE

10 to 30 grams per gallon-size batch (less for malty beers like Scottish and Abbey ales; more for super-hoppy IPAs and barleywines)

STORAGE

Not long! Hops spoil quickly when exposed to air, so store them in airtight containers and in the freezer.

SEE ALSO

Boil, page 36
Extra Hops, page 106

When you think about the flavor of craft beer, you're probably thinking about hops. But beer's most famous ingredient is also its newest.

Straight wort is sickeningly sweet (try it and see), so brewers have almost always mixed in herbs and spices. After ages of wild experimentation, brewers in the Middle Ages settled on gruit, a semi-secret mixture of yarrow, gale, and other herbs. (Learn to make your own on page 104). Mixing gruit was church business, and business was good—for centuries, bittering beer with anything else was illegal in parts of Europe. But as papal power waned in the 1500s, brewers branched out, and found hops.

First cultivated in the eighth century in the Hallertau region of southern Germany, hops are a climbing vine with green, conelike flowers full of citrusy, piney, bitter oils that brewers—and drinkers—love. (In fact, these days, male hops are often outlawed wherever female hops are grown—they'd pollinate the plant, and turn those cones into unusable seeds.) Hops grew quickly, packed all the punch of even the best gruit into one plant, and, best of all, weren't church property. They soon became the only spice that brewers used. Gruit was history. As a bonus, hops contain natural antibiotics that kept beer fresh along the web of trade routes starting to crisscross the continent—and beyond—in the 16th century. And so was born the IPA, or India Pale Ale, chock-full of hops to keep it fresh all the way to Bombay.

Hops vary dramatically in flavor based on where they're grown, and as cultivation spread across Europe—and, these days, into the U.S. and as far afield as China and New Zealand—different regional styles of beer followed. English pale ales show off the earthy notes of Kent-grown hops like Goldings and Fuggle; Czech pilsners get their kick from spicy Saaz; and our own West Coast IPAs would be nothing without the grapefruity tang of Amarillos and Cascades, grown in the Pacific Northwest. In fact, American craft beer is on the map these days thanks in part to those hop varieties, impossible to grow anywhere else. Before Prohibition, hops twisted through fields all over the U.S., centered mainly in California wine country and northern New York state. Today, Germany still leads the world in production, but American growers in Washington and Oregon's Yakima and Willamette valleys are catching up. (Help the cause! Learn how to grow your own hops on page 106.)

CHARACTERISTICS OF HOPS

Resin glands inside each hop cone contain a bitter substance called alpha acid. Boiling hops dissolves this acid into wort through a process called isomerization. But it gets even more complicated. Alpha acid has three component resins: humulone, adhumulone, and cohumulone. The percentages of each differ with variety and crop, but generally, more cohumulone means a rougher bitterness (hops such as Nugget and Cluster) and lower cohumulone means a softer bitterness (Saaz, Fuggle, Hallertau). More alpha acid in total makes for a more bitter hop. A hop's flavor and aroma, on the other hand, come from hop oils—which differ from acids in that boiling weakens and eventually destroys them.

Commercial brewers tend to talk about how beers and ingredients taste in terms of numbers. It's meant to be scientific, but to us, it's usually confusing. This is especially true with hops, since two varieties with the same basic stats can taste as different as geraniums and pine needles. Alpha acid content, measured as a percentage of weight, can give you a ballpark idea of what a hop will do to your beer. Lower levels make for subtler hops, like the famous "Noble Hops" of central Europe: Hallertau, Tettnanger, Spalt, and Saaz. (Think of the fresh, green aroma of a helles or a pilsner.) Resinous, tongue-coating high-alpha hops are the darlings of West Coast brewers, who use them in extra-bitter IPAs.

LUPULIN GLANDS

BRACT

BRACTEOLE

STRIG

Hops Flowers

The hop cone, or strobilus, is filled with tiny yellow sacks of resins and oils called "lupulin glands." These contain the flavoring and bittering compounds brewers use. The rest of the plant is a leafy vine, in the same biological family as cannabis.

A Hop by Any Other Name . . .

Four varieties of hops, prized for their delicate aroma, mild bitterness (that is, low cohumulone levels) and grown only in specific regions of Germany and the Czech Republic, are referred to as "Noble": Hallertau, Tettnanger, Spalt, and Saaz. The secret is in the soil. The red permian sandstone around Zatec, in the Czech Republic, for example, produces Saaz's spice. Of course, all hops are unique to where they're grown, and there's nothing inherently better about these four than any other. It's all in a name.

The higher a hop's alpha acid percentage (AA%), the higher a beer's IBUs, or International Bittering Units. One IBU is one part per million of isomerized alpha acid in a beer. Some imperial IPAs have hit the 100 IBU mark and beyond, but there's some debate as to whether anyone can actually taste differences at such high levels.

TYPES OF HOPS

The intricate mix of alpha acid resins and essential oils in hops determines when brewers use them, and for what purpose. Hops come in three varieties, bittering, dual-use (or flavoring), and aroma hops.

BITTERING HOPS The longer you boil hops, the more alpha acids you isomerize—and the bitterer your beer will be. Bittering hops are generally one-note hops with lots of alpha acid (9–18% AA) and fewer aromatic oils, so not much is lost by boiling the hell out of them. Brewers often add them right at the start of their boils.

DUAL-USE HOPS These hops have less alpha acid than bittering hops (4–8% AA), and can be used both for bittering and for aroma. When added about halfway into your boil, they contribute a little acid and a little oil. Brewers often use a combination of hops varieties at this stage to add complexity to their beer.

AROMA HOPS To draw out the delicate, citrusy notes of geraniol (in Cascade) or the richer spice of humulene (in Saaz), brewers add their aroma hops (also known as finishing hops) late in the boil to preserve their oils. Some brewers don't boil them at all, preferring to create aroma by dry-hopping (see page 106).

PRACTICAL ADVICE

WHOLE HOPS OR PELLET? Hops are dried before they're sold (although some breweries use them fresh off the vine) and either packaged as is or squashed into little pellets. Some brewers buy whole flower hops because the minimal processing leaves their resin glands intact. Others choose pellets for the same reason: Mashing up the hops breaks open the glands so the acids dissolve more easily in beer. Whole hops are a bit easier to filter out of your beer, but they suck up more wort in the process. We prefer the ease of using pellets—the taste difference is negligible.

BUYING HOPS Hops come vacuum-sealed, so it's impossible to smell them before you buy. Any self-respecting homebrew shop will try and sell the freshest hops it can, and if you end up taking home a stale batch, it'll likely replace it for you.

PREDICTING FLAVOR If you find a new hop but want to test its flavor before brewing, start by rubbing a pellet or cone between your palms to break it open and warm the oils. Is it harsh or mild? Floral, fruity, or grassy? Does it smell like cheese? If it does, chuck it—it's old and stale. You can also make a hop tea by steeping a few pellets in boiling water for a few minutes then straining them out. (It's rumored to help you sleep.) One brewery tests new hops by putting them in a vaporizer. Just make sure to clean it out first.

MAKING SUBSTITUTIONS Have a hop in mind but can't find it at the store? First, check the chart on the next page to see what's comparable in flavor. If you're using it for bittering purposes only, where flavor and aroma don't matter as much, find one with the same alpha acid content, or use this formula to make a substitution: AA % x grams (of desired hop) = AA % x grams (of substitute hop). Or, of course, you can just wing it.

STOCKING UP Keep hops in the freezer. If they're vacuum-packed, straight from the processing plant, they'll keep for a couple of years. Once opened, the clock starts ticking—use them within a month. Your freezer is probably full of nasty old food smells, so we'd recommend ziplocking your hops, then sealing the baggies in a big mason jar, just to be safe.

HOP KILLER
HOP ARMOR

Not Safe for Hops

Ever had skunky beer? If you drink the imported stuff in green bottles, you probably have. Why? Light. A particular wavelength of light vibrates certain hop molecules in such a way that they break apart into compounds pretty damn close to those in skunk spray. Brown bottles block those rays—which is why you'll reuse them for homebrew. Green or clear ones don't. You can see for yourself: Put a bottle of lager on a sunny windowsill for an hour and try it. Don't use Miller, though—they brew with a special hop extract that's been chemically altered not to go skunky.

FIELD GUIDE TO HOPS

How can one plant taste like so many? Based on where, when, and from what strain they're grown, hops can taste and smell like everything from mint to mangoes (to, if you're not careful, old cheese). So don't listen to those wine snobs—beer has terroir, too. On average, you'll hop your beer three times: once for bitterness, once for flavor, and once for aroma. We've arranged these hops accordingly, with bittering hops on the left, aroma hops on the right, and dual-use hops (which can serve as either) at the center. Of course, these are only guidelines. Even super-acidic varieties like Chinook and Simcoe aren't always out of place as aroma hops. And you can bitter with low-alpha acid hops like Kent Goldings and Saaz—you'll just need to use more of them. So don't take our word for it—try something new.

9-18% AA	4-8% AA	2-4% AA
BITTERING	**DUAL USE**	**AROMA**

EARTHY, GRASSY, MILD, RESINY, WOODY		
TARGET	FUGGLE GLACIER	KENT GOLDINGS STYRIAN GOLDINGS WILLAMETTE

HERBAL, MILDLY SPICY		
	HALLERTAU MT. HOOD VANGUARD	CRYSTAL HERSBRUCKER LIBERTY

MINTY, EVERGREEN		
	NORTHERN BREWER PERLE	

PINEY		
CHINOOK		

	BITTERING 9-18% AA	DUAL USE 4-8% AA	AROMA 2-4% AA
WALNUTTY, WOODY	SIMCOE		
HERBAL, SPICY, PUNGENT	COLUMBUS WARRIOR		
CITRUSY, GRAPEFRUITY, FLORAL	APOLLO CENTENNIAL SUMMIT	AHTANUM AMARILLO CASCADE	
LEMONY, BLACKCURRANT	SORACHI ACE		BRAMLING CROSS
TROPICAL FRUIT, MANGO, PINEAPPLE		CITRA	
MILDLY FRUITY, BLACKBERRY	GALENA PACIFIC GEM	BREWER'S GOLD PALISADE	
DELICATELY SPICY, CINNAMONY, FLORAL		CLUSTER STERLING SPALT	SAAZ TETTNANGER
NEUTRAL, CLEAN	MAGNUM NUGGET	CHALLENGER HORIZON NORTHDOWN	

YEAST

PRICE

$6 to $7 per tube (or "smack pack") of liquid yeast

USAGE

Each tube of yeast will brew up to four batches of beer, depending on the strength of the beer you're making

STORAGE

Always store your liquid yeast in the fridge, and be sure to use it before its "best by" date

SEE ALSO

Ferment, page 40
Sour Beers, page 114

Small as they are, the handling of yeast cells—those tiny critters that work by the billion turning wort into beer—can be the most complicated part of beer making. But don't worry. At its most basic, yeast is as simple as any other animal.

It needs to eat, breathe, and reproduce, and your job is to help it out. Going back to beer's earliest days, brewers had an inkling of what yeast was, or at least what it did, describing fermenting vats of beer as "boiling" or "talking." They just didn't know how it worked. Then in 1860, Louis Pasteur tagged the recently discovered yeast organism as the agent behind fermentation, and 25 years later Emil Christian Hansen finally captured a single cell of brewing yeast. There are thousands of kinds of yeasts on earth, but we're only concerned with Hansen's: brewing yeast, or genus *Saccharomyces*. It means sugar fungus, because that's what yeast is—single-celled mold that eats the sugar in beer to produce alcohol and carbon dioxide.

Traditional brewing yeast comes in two main groups: ale yeasts (*Saccharomyces cerevisiae*) typically make fuller-bodied, richer beers while lager yeasts (*Saccharomyces uvarum*, or sometimes *carlsbergensis*—yes, named after the brewery) make cleaner, lighter beers. There are exceptions of course: Anchor Steam is a dark, slightly fruity beer made with a lager yeast. But the distinction is grounded in truth. Ale yeasts like to ferment at warmer temperatures (55°F to 75°F and up), which produce the fruity chemical compounds called esters ales are known for. Lager yeasts, which originated in the chilly brewing caves of Germany, like it clean and cool (55°F and below).

You may hear that ale yeasts are "top-fermenting" and lager yeasts are "bottom-fermenting." Traditionally, that was true—ale yeasts would bubble up out of fermenters where brewers could harvest them and use them again (the Brits pioneered this method with the so-called "Burton Union" system), while lager yeasts stayed submerged. These days, though, a lot of ale yeasts work on the bottom too, so the distinction doesn't apply.

THE LIFE CYCLE OF YEAST

LAG (*A few hours*) As soon as yeast hits the wort, cells begin sucking up oxygen and amino acids to store as energy for reproduction and to build up their cell walls for fermentation. At this point, the cells are aerobic, which means they breathe oxygen.

GROWTH (*12 to 24 hours*) The yeast colony grows about five times in size, up to 50 million cells in each milliliter of wort. During this stage, yeast is still breathing oxygen and just starting to eat sugar. The cells turn glucose into an acid, which they oxidize into adenosine triphosphate, a source of energy (check your Chem-101 notes). The yeast also produces bad-tasting esters and a notoriously stinky molecule called diacetyl, but it'll scrub out these flavors in fermentation.

FERMENTATION (*2 to 6 days for ales, 4 to 10 days for lagers*) When there's no oxygen left, yeast stops turning glucose into energy and starts making booze. It begins by reducing the acids from its growth stage into carbon dioxide gas and long carbon molecules called acetaldehydes. Tack two hydrogen ions onto an acetaldehyde and you get ethyl alcohol. Ta-dah! If the yeast is fermenting too warm, or if it's battling wild contaminants, it might add too many ions and create fusel, or higher alcohols. You can taste them in some extra-strong beers: sweet and harsh or, on a bad day, almost nail-polish-y. Letting strong beers age will mellow these flavors. Fermentation finishes when the yeast just stops working, or when there are simply no sugars left for it to eat. You can tell it's over

WHITE LABS TUBE **WYEAST SMACK PACK**

Tube or Activator?

Two major companies make liquid yeast: White Labs, who package theirs in test tube–like plastic vials; and Wyeast, who use smack packs. Smack packs are plastic bags of yeast with a smaller bag of wort inside them. Pop the wort bag, and the yeast wakes up and starts to grow. Let the bag puff up, and it's ready to pitch into your wort. Vials just need to be brought up to room temperature and be given a good shake.

when your beer's gravity, or density, stops decreasing. This means no more sugars are being converted into less-dense alcohol. The "higher attenuating" a strain is, the more sugars it can chew through before it tires out, and the drier the beer it will make.

SEDIMENTATION (*3 to 5 days*) After fermenting your beer, yeast begins to flocculate, or settle out. The colony falls to the bottom of the fermenter and goes dormant. After about a month, the cells will begin to eat each other in a cannibalistic process called autolysis that can make your beer taste a little like Vegemite. Lagers and strong beers like barleywines that require more than a month to condition should be siphoned off this sediment and into a secondary fermenter, before long-term aging.

TYPES OF YEAST

Yeast comes either dried or as a liquid. Liquid yeast doesn't store as long as dry yeast—only a few weeks once opened instead of a year or more—but it's generally healthier than the dried stuff, and comes in dozens more varieties. If you can find only dry yeast, that's okay, but it needs to be rehydrated before you add it. Boil 1 cup of water to sanitize it, let it cool to 80°F, and sprinkle in a packet of yeast. Let it sit for 15 minutes, then pitch into your wort.

HOW MUCH TO USE Theoretically, you could add a single yeast cell to your wort and it would divide itself and reproduce into a colony big enough to ferment all the sugars. But to make things easier on the yeast cells (they can put off bad flavors when overworked) and to start a quick fermentation that keeps any other invading bacteria at bay, you should pitch, or pour in, a lot.

Tubes and pouches hold 100 billion yeast cells; dried packets, only 60 billion. How many cells to pitch depends on how strong a beer you're making. For an average-strength ale with an original gravity of anything up to 1.049, pitch 30 billion cells. That's about one-third of a tube or smack pack (or half a packet of rehydrated dried yeast). You can save the rest in a sanitized jelly jar in the fridge. It will take 60 billion cells to ferment stronger stuff up to 1.079. If you're going even bigger than that, use 70 billion cells or more. Because lager yeasts have to work in colder temperatures, you'll have to pitch more cells—use about twice as much yeast in a lager as you would in an ale.

You may hear about yeast starters. This is a way to grow a store-bought container of yeast up to the amount you need to ferment your beer by feeding it sterilized wort in increasing amounts over a few days. This is really necessary only if you're making many gallons of beer at a time, and even then, only if you're having trouble with slow or inefficient fermentations. Since you're making one-gallon batches, don't worry about it!

FERMENTATION TEMPERATURE

Different yeasts prefer different temperatures. Most ale yeasts like things to be between 65°F and 70°F, but a few strains—like saison yeasts—work best in greater heat, even as high as 90°F. Lager yeasts prefer things 55°F or cooler—or else they'll make beer that tastes way too fruity for crisper styles like pilsners.

Hitting and maintaining these exact temperatures can be tough. Find a closet away from windows or radiators—or, better yet, a basement. It's most important to keep things even. Wild temperature fluctuations can stress out your yeast more than a fermentation that's consistently a few degrees warmer or cooler than the ideal. If your place is just too hot—or its temperatures too erratic—you can soup up a mini-fridge, using a plug-in temperature controller, and ferment your beer within a steady range (see page 162).

Use a sanitized—or better, an infrared (see page 163)—thermometer to check your beer's temperature while it's fermenting. It's a good idea to record these measurements, because off flavors in finished beer can often be traced back to fermentation temperature. Don't worry too much, though. California Commons, like Anchor Steam, are brewed with lager yeast at ale temperatures, and they're delicious.

ORIGINAL GRAVITY	AMOUNT
1.030 – 1.039	¼ tube
1.040 – 1.049	⅓ tube
1.050 – 1.079	½ tube
1.080 – 1.099	⅔ tube
1.100 – 1.120	¾ tube

Gravity and Yeast

Your hydrometer (see page 41) can be your best brewing partner. Use it often, and try not to drop it. Measure your wort's gravity before you add yeast to see how much yeast you'll need to pitch to ferment those sugars (see above). Then, as your beer ferments, take a gravity reading every couple of days to check its progress. When the gravity stops dropping, your yeast has stopped eating sugar, and it's time to bottle—or, if you're brewing a big beer, condition in a secondary fermenter.

FIELD GUIDE TO YEAST

We like using White Labs tubes because it's easy to sanitize a sealed tube, measure out just enough yeast to ferment our small batches, then reseal the tube and stash it in the fridge for the next brew day. Any yeast will ferment your beer, as long as it's fresh, but different strains create different flavors. In general, British ale yeasts are a bit fruity; Belgian yeasts even more so; American yeasts are crisper; and lager yeasts—often German—are clean and dry. There are dozens of substyles to choose from—we like making two or more batches of the same recipe, then fermenting each with a different yeast.

Beer styles to try with this strain

PALE ALE · WHEAT BEER · BROWN ALE · SAISON · PORTER · ABBEY ALE · STOUT · PILSNER · SCOTTISH ALE · BARLEY-WINE

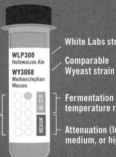

WLP300
Hefeweizen Ale
WY3068
Weihenstephan Weizen

68–72°F

MEDIUM

White Labs strain

Comparable Wyeast strain

Fermentation temperature range

Attenuation (low, medium, or high)

WLP001
California Ale
WY1056
American Ale

68–73°F

HIGH

WLP002
English Ale
WY1968
London ESB Ale

65–68°F

LOW

WLP013
London Ale
WY1028
London Ale

66–71°F

MEDIUM

WLP028
Edinburgh Scottish Ale
WY1728
Scottish Ale

65–70°F

MEDIUM

BRITISH STRAINS

WLP400
Belgianwit Ale

WY3944
Belgian Witbier

67–74°F

MEDIUM

WLP566
Belgian Saison II

68–78°F

HIGH

WLP566
Abbey Ale

WY3787
Trappist High
Gravity

66–72°F

HIGH

WLP550
Belgian Ale

WY3522
Belgian Ardennes

68–78°F

HIGH

WLP300
Hefeweizen Ale

WY3068
Weihenstephan
Weizen

68–72°F

MEDIUM

WLP029
German Ale/
Kölsch

63–69°F

HIGH

WLP800
Pilsner Lager

WY2001
Urquell

50–55°F

MEDIUM

WLP810
San Francisco
Lager

WY2112
California Lager

58–65°F

LOW

JOHN MAIER

BREWMASTER, ROGUE ALES

You grow your own hops, but you also grow and malt your own barley, which seems even more unusual.

We have a floor malting facility, and that's pretty rare. [Floor malting is a 19th-century practice of germinating malt on a heated wooden floor and rotating the grains with rakes.] I used to be able to get it from England, but not many people malt that way anymore. There's just something about it, turning the grains by hand, it really feels homegrown.

You make dozens of beers, way more than most other breweries your size. Where do you keep getting ideas?

I get a lot from homebrewers. I go to competitions, taste beers, ask people questions. Sometimes people who brew with our house yeast will send me recipes. [Hazelnut Nectar was based on a homebrewer's recipe.] But I've been doing this for 23 years. At this point it's 10 percent brain, 90 percent heart. I'll wake up in the middle of the night with an idea for a beer.

Does brewing from the heart, and making so many recipes, ever get you into trouble?

Variety is the spice of life! But it is hard to get everything out on time. We use our brewpubs in Eugene and Portland to test recipes, but I have to make sure I get it right. One time, I wanted to re-release a Scotch ale we hadn't brewed since 1998. And I lost the recipe. Thankfully a guy in the warehouse had it scribbled in an old notepad. I thought, Okay, I think I can make something out of this. And I did.

Is that you on the bottles?

No, that's a fictitious guy. I'm on one, the Maierfest. I used to be on the Maierbock, which became Dead Guy. We brewed it for a restaurant in Portland, and the owner changed the name and gave it the skeleton logo. The new logo made it popular. I even changed the beer— I started using an ale yeast instead of a lager yeast. But nobody seemed to notice.

Your nickname is "More Hops."

Yeah, well, I use a lot of hops. I've made a career out of it. I've gotten more malty as I've grown older, though.

NEWPORT, OREGON

EST. 1988

SIZE: 85,000 barrels/year

OUR FAVORITES: Chipotle Ale, Double Mocha Porter, Chatoe Rogue series

They might answer their phone with, "Rogue Nation World Headquarters," but Newport, Oregon's Rogue is defiantly homegrown. In 1989, founders Jack Joyce, Bob Woodell, Rob Strasser, and Jeff Schultz moved their year-old brewery into a Newport garage offered to them by the chowder house next door in exchange for a promise to brew for locals first. When a bad European harvest in 2007 made hop prices shoot up, Rogue planted 42 acres of their own. They couldn't tell their brewmaster, John "More Hops" Maier—an Oregon native himself—to use less. John brews locally and sustainably (down to Rogue's "free-range water"), but there's nothing precious about it. Rogue doesn't speak French: they call it "dirt-oir." From their bold labels outside to the big beers inside, Rogue dares you to tell them otherwise.

Chapter Two — — **MAKE**

TEN **GREAT RECIPES** AND **BONUS STEPS**

THE FLAVOR BALLPARK

Categorizing beers is tough. Part science (alpha acids, ABV), part palate—and just when you think you have a style pegged, some brewer comes up with a new take on it. Still, we have to try! This chart puts the 10 basic recipes that follow in the bitter-vs-sweet ballpark. If you're willing to get creative, where they'll land is up to you.

There are hundreds of beer styles out there, but just as beer itself can be broken down into only four ingredients, most styles of beer come from a few basic families. There are exceptions, of course—like sour beers, which we'll get to later—but for the most part, any beer you'd want to make starts with one of these basic recipes.

So we've kept them simple: delicious as is, but perfect foundations for building something new. They're arranged—loosely—in terms of difficulty. Any recipe here is beginner-friendly, but if you jump right into a dry-hopped, kumquat-infused imperial Belgian witbier and something turns out a little off, you'll have a harder time pinpointing what went wrong if you haven't brewed a simple pale ale first. Once you're comfortable, throw off the training wheels, and let 'er rip!

There's no Reinheitsgebot here in America, but for most of the last century you wouldn't have known it—beer was invariably bland, fizzy, and yellow. In the past 30 years, though, craft brewers have giddily taken basic beers (like the 10 recipes here) and run wild with them. Today, we don't just have pale ales and porters, but imperial IPAs, chocolate-coffee stouts, and barrel-aged—well, everything.

Beer is always changing, and the beauty of brewing on a small scale is that you get to change it whenever—and however—you want.

READING A RECIPE When reading our recipes, first learn a little about the history of each style, and how craft brewers are reinterpreting it today. We'll give you general guidelines for which malt, hops, and yeast to use to make a basic version of the beer, tasting suggestions for American takes on the style, and ideas for brewing some of our favorite variations. We'll explain those experiments in more detail later in the chapter with the help of some of today's most creative brewers. So consider the information that follows as suggestions—there's more than one way to hop a beer. Take inspiration wherever you find it, and remember, beer is boring only if you make it that way.

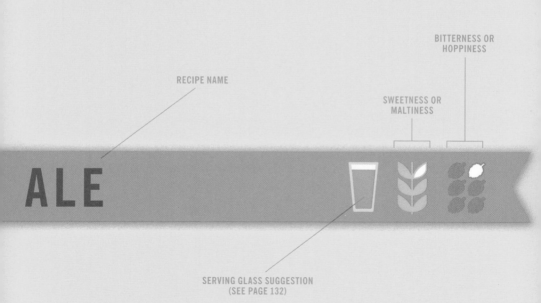

BITTERNESS OR HOPPINESS

SWEETNESS OR MALTINESS

RECIPE NAME

ALE

SERVING GLASS SUGGESTION (SEE PAGE 132)

① MASH

GRAINS	AMOUNT (wt)
Base malt	2–4 lb
Flavor, crystal, or roasted malt	5–15 oz
Specialty grains or adjuncts	5–10 oz
Bring 4–10 qt strike water to 163°F / Mash for 60 min at	140–158°F

These are the grains you'll use. Weigh them out together, and add them to your mash water as explained on page 32.

② SPARGE

Target pre-boil gravity:	1.025–1.065

Measure your beer's gravity often, starting as soon as you sparge. This will give you a sense of whether you're on the right track to the strength specified by the style. A couple points of variation is fine.

③ BOIL

HOP VARIETY	ALPHA ACID	AMOUNT (g)	BOIL TIME
Bittering addition	3–12 %	10–30 g	60 min
Flavor addition	3–12 %	0–30 g	5–20 min
Aroma addition	3–12 %	0–10 g	1 min

These are your hops. Set them out before you boil, and toss them in at the times specified.

④ CHILL

Target original gravity:	1.040–1.105

⑤ FERMENT

YEAST STRAIN	AMOUNT	TEMPERATURE	FERMENTATION
Yeast style (White Labs #)	⅓ – 1 tube	°F	2–4 weeks
	Target final gravity:		1.010–1.025

Be sure to watch your beer's temperature and gravity as it ferments. It's ready to bottle when its gravity stops falling—usually when it reaches the target final gravity, and usually within the amount of time specified. Fluctuations do happen.

⑥ BOTTLE

Bottling sugar:	17–28 g

🜂 EXPERIMENT

Experimental Ale: Tweak this basic recipe by trying one of the dozens of experimental techniques covered on pages 100 to 115. We make some specific suggestions, but really it's all up to you!

Check the experiment box for tips on how to make this beer your own.

PALE ALE

As ubiquitous as pale ale is these days, its origins are surprisingly upper-crust. For centuries, all malts were kilned over wood fires, which turned the grains—and the resulting beers—dark and toasty. Maltsters started using coal in about 1850, creating paler malts and the possibility for beer that was bright, clear, and very expensive. Appreciating the color and clarity required drinking pale ale out of glasses—not the standard, opaque ceramic or tin mugs of the day—and glass was pricey too. As pale ale became cheaper and easier to make, 19th-century Londoners embraced it. They divided and subdivided it into multiple categories: bitters; special or best bitters; extra-special bitters; and, of course, the India Pale Ale.

American brewers have defined the pale ale market since the 1980s, and the distinctions continue with double, imperial, and even Belgian pale ales. But the IPA, that most delicious vestige of the British Empire, still reigns. Originally brewed for the officer class of the British Army stationed in swanky south Asia, IPAs were packed with hops to preserve them during the long voyage south. Unlike many IPAs today, the first of these brews were typically weaker than standard pale ales, since more alcohol means more sugars, which are more likely to spoil. Today they can be the biggest beers on the shelf, but back then, IPAs were considered light.

MALT Start light: American 2-Row for a drier flavor; Maris Otter for something a little maltier—then add just a touch of light crystal malt or flavor malt. Two to 6 ounces of 20°L Crystal, Munich, or Vienna malt works well.

HOPS Citrusy American pales are typically hopped with Cascade or Chinook. Mellower, floral British pales use Kent Goldings or Fuggle. Changing your hop profile is a great way to experiment with this style. Follow the lead of some great American craft brewers and try dry-hopping, wet-hopping, or late-wort hopping with an aromatic, experimental strain. (See page 106.)

YEAST Pale ales generally don't have much yeast character, since you want the flavor of the hops to shine through. California Ale yeast is the standard high-attenuating strain used to brew drier versions. London Ale is a good choice for slightly maltier pales. Experiment with Belgian Ale strains for even more complex flavors.

ORIGINAL GRAVITY 1.040–1.060 (and as high as 1.090 for imperial IPAs)

STRENGTH 4–10% ABV

BEERS TO TRY *American*: Sierra Nevada Pale Ale, Oskar Blues Dale's Pale Ale. *English-style*: Brooklyn Pennant Ale, Firestone Walker Double Barrel Ale. *IPA*: Ballast Point Sculpin, Bell's Two-Hearted Ale, Stone IPA, Bear Republic Racer 5. *Double IPA*: Russian River Pliny the Elder, Lagunitas Maximus, Dogfish Head 90-Minute. *Belgian-style IPA*: Great Divide Belgica, Green Flash Le Freak.

① MASH

GRAINS	AMOUNT (wt)
American 2-Row malt	2 lb 4 oz
20°L Crystal malt	4 oz
Bring 5 qt strike water to 163°F / Mash for 60 min at	153°F

◀ American 2-Row makes a cleaner, lighter pale ale. Replace the 2-Row with British Pale Ale malt or Maris Otter malt for a richer taste. If you like a drier version—like Sierra Nevada Pale Ale—eliminate the Crystal malt.

② SPARGE

Target pre-boil gravity: 1.035

③ BOIL

HOP VARIETY	ALPHA ACID	AMOUNT (g)	BOIL TIME
Cascade	6 %	20 g	60 min
Cascade	6 %	10 g	20 min
Cascade	6 %	10 g	1 min

◀ Cascade is a classic American aroma hop, with characteristic notes of grapefruit and geranium. Start with a simple hop profile like this for your first batch, then go wild!

④ CHILL

Target original gravity: 1.055

⑤ FERMENT

YEAST STRAIN	AMOUNT	TEMPERATURE	FERMENTATION
California Ale (WLP001)	½ tube	68°F	2 weeks
		Target final gravity:	1.012

◀ Yeast notes should be minimal for this style—it's all about hops—but using a lager yeast like San Francisco Lager (WLP810) then fermenting at your regular temperature gets you a so-called California Common like Anchor Steam.

⑥ BOTTLE

Bottling sugar: 22 g

🧪 EXPERIMENT

IPA: Double the bittering hops, then try late-wort hopping or dry-hopping. *See page 106.*

Imperial IPA: Add 1 lb 8 oz base malt to the mash, then double all the hop additions.

Black IPA: Add 4 oz Carafa malt to the mash, then hop as you would an IPA.

Belgian Pale: Use a Belgian yeast strain and ferment warmer, as you would an Abbey Ale. *See page 92.*

BROWN ALE

Brown ale was the first commercially produced beer style in England. In its day—before pales, before stouts—brown ale was all there was. The key ingredient was brown malt, kilned lightly over a hardwood fire, which gave the ale a nutty and slightly caramelized flavor.

In Britain, browns were sometimes called "running beers" and sold fresh, straight from the brewery. (Old, sour browns were sold as porter.) Brown ales and milds are two versions of the same basic beer, divided more by tradition than taste. Browns originated in northern England, and tend to be lighter and stronger than milds. Newcastle is a northern brown, Cooper's Dark is a southern-style mild.

American browns, like their English cousins, are brewed with lightly kilned malts for their signature color—but then aggressively hopped and fermented with cleaner yeasts to let those flavors shine. Like most American versions of British beers, they also tend to be stronger. There's a rumor the style was invented by a cadre of hop-head Texans, but whatever its origins, it brought brown malt—once impossible to find—into homebrew shops for good.

MALT Mostly British Pale Ale malt, which has a richer, breadier flavor than American 2-Row. Add about a half pound of Brown malt, or a combination of Brown and Crystal, which is a bit sweeter, or any other lightly toasted malts. An ounce of Chocolate malt will give it a roasted aroma (Black Patent or Roasted Barley are stronger). An ounce of Wheat malt helps with body and head retention.

HOPS No surprises: Kent Goldings and Fuggle are traditional for English brown ales; Cascade, Amarillo, and Centennial for American.

YEAST London Ale yeast and other British strains tend to leave your beer a bit sweeter, which is good for maltier browns. If you want a drier, hoppier profile, switch to California Ale yeast. For a more complex and slighty fruity character, try a Belgian strain.

ORIGINAL GRAVITY 1.045–1.065

STRENGTH 4.5–6.5% ABV

BEERS TO TRY *American*: Smuttynose Old Dog, Avery Ellie's Brown, Cigar City Maduro Oatmeal Brown, Brooklyn Brown, Dogfish Head Indian Brown Ale, Sixpoint Brownstone.

① MASH

GRAINS	AMOUNT (wt)
Pale Ale malt	2 lb 4 oz
Brown malt	4 oz
40°L Crystal malt	4 oz
Chocolate malt	1 oz
Wheat malt	1 oz
Bring 5 qt strike water to 163°F / Mash for 60 min at	153°F

◀ Pale Ale malt is a tiny bit richer than American 2-Row. The Brown and Chocolate malts (which are both malted then kilned at high temperatures) give brown ale its characteristic color and roasted, nutty flavor.

② SPARGE

Target pre-boil gravity: 1.040

③ BOIL

HOP VARIETY	ALPHA ACID	AMOUNT (g)	BOIL TIME
Horizon	11 %	10 g	60 min
Cascade	6 %	5 g	20 min
Amarillo	7 %	5 g	1 min

◀ Horizon is a neutral bittering hop. Cascade and Amarillo contribute classic American hop character—floral and citrusy.

④ CHILL

Target original gravity: 1.065

⑤ FERMENT

YEAST STRAIN	AMOUNT	TEMPERATURE	FERMENTATION
English Ale (WLP002)	½ tube	65°F	2 weeks
		Target final gravity:	1.020

◀ California Ale yeast is the traditional strain for drier American brown ales. We like English Ale yeast because it has a lower attenuation and makes a sweeter, maltier beer. London Ale yeast produces a beer somewhere in the middle.

⑥ BOTTLE

Bottling sugar: 22 g

🧪 EXPERIMENT

Nut Brown Ale: Add ¼ cup ground, roasted nuts to your mash. *See page 105.*
House-Roasted Brown: Roast your own Brown malt. *See page 101.*

PORTER

Industrialized brewing began with porter. In the 1700s, beer was mostly brown, and often sour and stale. Savvy pub-goers knew to cut old beer's funk by mixing it with fresher stuff in blends called "half-and-half" or "three-threads." In 1722, George Harwood took a shortcut and brewed the first "whole butt," or pre-made blend (butt meant barrel)—and the porter craze was on.

Brewing porter required storing beer in vats until it got sour enough to blend with new beer and sell. The porter boom in the early 1800s led to bigger and bigger vats; one was huge enough to hold a 200-person dinner in. Soon, big brewers began switching to pale malts from the less efficient brown, and making up the color with caramelized sugar. When black malt was invented in 1817, they switched again. That made porters and stouts even closer cousins, and these days they're often indistinguishable, since both may be plenty strong.

Thanks to their solid backbone—heavier than a brown but not as biting and rich as a stout—porters are great for experimenting. If you're itching to play around with coffee, chocolate, fruits, or spices, this is your style.

MALT Mix a big American 2-Row malt base (at least 2 lb) with 6 or 7 ounces of Crystal or Munich malt, and a little less roasted malt (like Coffee or Chocolate). Adding an ounce or two of Roasted Barley or Black Patent malt darkens the color towards stout territory. Experiment by adding some smoked malt to emphasize the roasted malts' already rich aroma.

HOPS In England, as with brown ales, Fuggle and Goldings are classic. In America, dry-hopped porters are not unheard of, and as always, the stronger you make it, the more bittering hops you'll want to use for balance.

YEAST British yeasts will give your porter a slightly fruity character that works well alongside rich malts. American yeasts brew a cleaner, brighter beer.

ORIGINAL GRAVITY 1.050–1.070

STRENGTH 5–7% ABV

BEERS TO TRY *American*: Deschutes Black Butte Porter, Yuengling Porter, Anchor Porter, Great Lakes Edmund Fitzgerald. *Smoked*: Alaskan Smoked Porter, Stone Smoked Porter. *Chocolate/Coffee*: Rogue Mocha Porter, Maui Brewing Coconut Porter, Sixpoint Gorilla Warfare.

① MASH

GRAINS	AMOUNT (wt)
American 2-Row malt	2 lb 4 oz
60°L Crystal malt	6 oz
Caramunich malt	4 oz
Coffee malt	4 oz
Black Patent malt	2 oz

Bring 6 qt strike water to 163°F / Mash for 60 min at | 153°F

◀ Add a few ounces of oatmeal (toasted in your oven) for a breadier, cookie-dough porter. See page 102.

② SPARGE

Target pre-boil gravity: 1.044

③ BOIL

HOP VARIETY	ALPHA ACID	AMOUNT (g)	BOIL TIME
Northern Brewer	8 %	20 g	60 min
Cascade	6 %	5 g	1 min

④ CHILL

Target original gravity: 1.063

⑤ FERMENT

YEAST STRAIN	AMOUNT	TEMPERATURE	FERMENTATION
London Ale (WLP013)	½ tube	66°F	2 weeks

Target final gravity: 1.020

◀ Switching to California Ale yeast will produce a drier beer, and highlight the Cascade aroma hops.

⑥ BOTTLE

Bottling sugar: 22 g

◀ After bottling and carbonating, you'll want to age your porters for at least a month or two, giving those dark, toasty malts some time to mellow out. And this beer will only get better over time. (Dark malts are delicious and complex but can taste a bit acrid when your beer is still young.)

⚗ EXPERIMENT

Smoked Porter: Add a few ounces or up to 1 lb smoked malt to your mash. *See page 100.*
Sour Porter: Add ¼ tube brettanomyces (wild yeast) to a secondary fermenter. *See page 115.*
Pumpkin Porter: Add a small pumpkin, halved and oven-roasted, to your mash. *See page 108.*

STOUT

Though it's as iconic a style these days as pale ale, stout was an adjective before it was a beer. At first, "stout" just referred to a strong porter. Then, in 1817, British maltsters cranked up their kilns and invented Black Patent malt and Roasted Barley, opening brewers up to even darker beers.

Guinness is the classic dry stout. Made with roasted barley to sneak around a tax on malted grain, it's characteristically sharp and dry. (Roasted barley is unmalted, and therefore sugar-free). A stronger version of their Irish Dry Stout, the Guinness Extra Stout Porter, was made for export and became a favorite in the Caribbean. Pretty soon brewers there made their own: The excellent Dragon Stout is one.

Not so in Czarist Russia, where Catherine II and her court stuck with the heavily hopped imperial stouts the British sent her. Back in England, weaker stouts—in particular sweet or milk stouts made with lactose sugar—were prescribed by the quart to invalids and pregnant women.

As with porters, American brewers go nuts with their stouts, adding spices and fruits, aging them in barrels, and, of course, cranking up the booze. Mother's milk they are not.

MALT Maris Otter makes a good base malt here: It's slightly biscuity with just the hint of sweetness you need to balance the darker grains. Go easy on the dark-roasted stuff—2 to 5 ounces will give enough bite. Unlike a porter, you don't want a lot of sweetness in a dry stout, so this recipe cuts out Crystal malt altogether. If you're brewing a stronger, sweeter, or spicier stout, you'll want to add some Crystal malt back in.

HOPS Your focus here should be on bitterness, not aroma. You can make a dry stout by boiling all your hops for the full 60 minutes. Challenger and Target are typical English bittering hops; Cascade and Chinook are the American choices. Stronger stouts can stand an additional flavor or aroma addition, and can also be dry-hopped.

YEAST Use Irish Ale yeast for a traditional dry stout, or London Ale if you want it a bit sweeter (our preference). If you make an imperial stout, you'll want to use something stronger, like the clean California Ale strain.

ORIGINAL GRAVITY 1.050–1.075 (higher for imperials)

STRENGTH 5–7% ABV

BEERS TO TRY *American*: Chelsea Black Hole Stout. *Oatmeal*: Rogue Shakespeare Oatmeal Stout. *Coffee*: Troegs Java Head, AleSmith Speedway Stout. *Chocolate*: Brooklyn Black Chocolate Stout. *Imperial*: Great Divide Yeti, Deschutes Abyss, Stone Imperial Russian Stout.

1 MASH

GRAINS	AMOUNT (wt)
Maris Otter malt	2 lb
Roasted Barley	4 oz
Flaked Wheat	2 oz

Bring 5 qt strike water to 163°F / Mash for 60 min at	153°F

◀ When you experiment with this style, first give it a richer foundation by adding a full pound of Maris Otter base malt plus 4 oz of Crystal malt, and replace the Flaked Wheat with 4 oz of Chocolate malt. Then take it from there.

2 SPARGE

Target pre-boil gravity:	1.033

3 BOIL

HOP VARIETY	ALPHA ACID	AMOUNT (g)	BOIL TIME
Target	9.5 %	20 g	60 min

◀ Stouts are relatively bitter, but they don't have a lot of hop flavor and aroma, so load up on hops early in the boil. If you're messing around with fruits and spices, adding 5 g of flavor and aroma hops will balance things out.

4 CHILL

Target original gravity:	1.053

5 FERMENT

YEAST STRAIN	AMOUNT	TEMPERATURE	FERMENTATION
London Ale (WLP013)	½ tube	66°F	2 weeks

Target final gravity:	1.015

6 BOTTLE

Bottling sugar:	17 g

◀ To get a creamier body for your stout, add less bottling sugar than you would for a lighter beer—about three-quarters as much as you use for a pale ale.

EXPERIMENT

Chocolate Stout: Add 3 oz cocoa powder at the end of the boil. *See page 105.*

Coffee Stout: Pour your wort into the fermenter through a hopback filled with 20 g ground coffee beans. *See page 105.*

Hot-Pepper Stout: Add ¼ oz chopped, dried peppers at the end of the boil. *See page 104.*

SCOTTISH ALE

Brewing in Scotland dates back to the Celts, who flavored pretty much everything with heather. Beer was a ceremonial drink, probably helped along by a hallucinogenic moss, called fogg, that can grow on the heather flowers.

When the English down below started using hops in the 1700s, the Scots resisted, for tradition's sake, and for climate's. Barley grows great in the Scottish countryside; hops don't grow at all. Plus, Scottish brewers were exempt from a 17th-century English tax on malt. Their beer, then, became sticky-sweet, often smoky from roasting malt over peat fires, and was flavored with everything but hops: heather, of course, as well as ginger, pepper, meadowsweet, and an ingredient of early insecticides called quassia. Anything was better than asking the Brits for some Kent Goldings. Hops show up these days, but their influence is minimal.

Scottish beer is divided into often confused—and confusing—labels based on strength and how much a pint used to cost: 60-shilling, or light ale; 70-shilling, or heavy; 80-shilling, or export; and 90–160-shilling, also called Scotch ale, or "wee heavy." "Wee" referred to the size of the serving glass, not the strength of the beer.

MALT Maris Otter is the traditional base malt for Scottish beers. Add to that a variety of sweet, biscuity specialty grains to round out the beer's malt character. Add a pinch of Roasted Barley for toasty notes or Peated malt for some smoke. Mash relatively hot to get a thick, dextrinous wort of long-chain sugars your yeast won't eat. This will help it stay sweet.

HOPS Hops are only for bittering here, so it's a good chance to clean out your freezer. Toss in the oldest hops you have. If you're buying fresh pellets, mild hops like Fuggle, Kent Goldings, and Willamette are good choices.

YEAST Look for a yeast with low esters—you want your malt to do all the talking. Scottish Ale yeast is the traditional strain, but Irish Ale and California Ale strains are also good options. Ferment cool at 65°F. After you bottle, stash your beers way back in the fridge and forget about them for as long as you can. This malt-heavy beer benefits from cold-storage for about 3 months (and closer to 6 months for a wee heavy).

ORIGINAL GRAVITY 1.030–1.045 (and 1.070–1.130 for strong Scotch ales)

STRENGTH 60-shillings can be as low as 2.5%, while Scotch ales go as high as 10% ABV

BEERS TO TRY Oskar Blues Old Chub, Long Trail Hibernator, AleSmith Wee Heavy, Great Divide Claymore, Founders Dirty Bastard

① MASH

GRAINS	AMOUNT (wt)
Maris Otter malt	1 lb 4 oz
60°L Crystal malt	4 oz
120°L Crystal malt	2 oz
Aromatic malt	2 oz
Honey malt	2 oz
Roasted Barley	½ oz

Bring 4 qt strike water to 168°F / Mash for 60 min at **158°F**

◀ This is a recipe for 70-shilling Scottish Ale. For a 120-shilling Scotch Ale use 3 lb total Maris Otter. For even lighter fare, cut the Maris Otter down to a mere 14 oz—but keep the specialty grain build the same.

② SPARGE

Target pre-boil gravity: **1.025**

◀ Mashing at this higher temperature creates some longer-chain sugars that the yeast won't be able to eat and will leave behind for you, making for a sweeter, maltier—and traditionally Scottish—ale.

③ BOIL

HOP VARIETY	ALPHA ACID	AMOUNT (g)	BOIL TIME
Fuggle	5 %	15 g	60 min

④ CHILL

Target original gravity: **1.040**

◀ Mild English hops contribute a little bitterness for balance, but very little hop flavor—which, in this case, is a good thing.

⑤ FERMENT

YEAST STRAIN	AMOUNT	TEMPERATURE	FERMENTATION
Scottish Ale (WLP028)	⅓ tube	65°F	2 weeks

Target final gravity: **1.012**

◀ Scottish Ale yeast is relatively clean-tasting and has a low attenuation, which means it leaves behind some sugars and makes for a maltier beer. The stronger your beer, the longer you'll want to ferment it, and the more yeast you'll need to pitch. Think 3 weeks—and up to a full tube—for a Strong Scotch Ale.

⑥ BOTTLE

Bottling sugar: **17 g**

🧪 EXPERIMENT

Heather Ale: Replace the hops with 1½ cups heather tips. *See page 104.*

Smoked Scottish Ale: Add 6–12 oz smoked or peated malt to your mash. *See page 100.*

WHEAT BEER

Wheat beers come in three traditional varieties: Belgian witbier, Bavarian weizen (or weissbier), and Berliner weisse. All three, to keep it simple, are brewed with mostly Wheat malt and are fermented with a fruity yeast that is often left unfiltered in the bottle.

Bavarian weizen is from Munich, where the Degenberger royal family held the exclusive license to make it. (They brewed outside the law: Wheat beer is the only exception to Germany's Reinheitsgebot.) Bavarian weissbier slowly lost popularity until the royal family finally ceded its rights in 1872 and Georg Schneider scooped them up. The beer he started making, Schneider-weiss, is still one of the best. Weissbier comes filtered (kristalweizen) or unfiltered (hefeweizen), and is technically unspiced—its characteristic pepper, clove, and banana notes come from the yeast alone.

Berliners made their wheat beer a bit differently. Brewers there didn't boil their wort at all, and so the unsanitized beer spoiled quickly, giving Berliner weisse its acidic tang. Some like it that way (Napoleon's army called it "the champagne of the north"); others take theirs with a shot of flavored syrup to cut the sourness.

Witbier, Belgium's spiced version, was dead by the 1950s, and would have remained so if Pierre Celis hadn't opened his Hoegaarde, Belgium, brewery in 1965 to make only that style. Now Hoegaarden is synonymous with wheat beer—and owned by Anheuser-Busch.

American brewers pick influences from all three. Their wheat beers are often spiced, but richer and maltier and—we hope—served sans orange slice.

MALT Simple: Half of your grist should be Wheat malt, and the rest either Pilsner malt or American 2-Row.

HOPS Hallertau and Saaz are traditional, but hop notes are minimal, so experiment! Lagunitas's Little Sumpin' Sumpin' is a great dry-hopped American wheat beer.

YEAST An estery yeast strain, fermented warm, is what gives wheat beer its famous banana and bubble-gum flavors. If that's not your thing, keep your fermentation cooler, around 65°F. For American wheat beer, try the cleaner American Hefe strain or even a Kölsch yeast.

ORIGINAL GRAVITY 1.040–1.055. Berliner weisse is on the lower end, closer to 1.030.

STRENGTH 4–5.5% ABV

BEERS TO TRY *American*: Bell's Oberon, Firestone Walker Solace, Lagunitas Little Sumpin' Sumpin'. *Weizen*: Sierra Nevada Kellerweis Hefeweizen. *Berliner weisse*: The Bruery Hottenroth. *Witbier*: Jolly Pumpkin Calabaza Blanca, Leelanau Whaleback White, Ommegang Witte, Great Lakes Holy Moses, Allagash White, Great Divide Double Wit.

① MASH

GRAINS	AMOUNT (wt)
Belgian Pilsner malt	1 lb
Wheat malt	1 lb
Bring 4 qt strike water to 163°F / Mash for 60 min at	153°F

◀ This recipe is for a traditional German hefeweizen. To make a dunkelweizen or a weizenbock (both dark wheat beers), add 8 oz of darker malts to your mash: Try a combination of Crystal malt, Munich malt, Chocolate malt, and Special B malt.

② SPARGE

Target pre-boil gravity: 1.029

③ BOIL

HOP VARIETY	ALPHA ACID	AMOUNT (g)	BOIL TIME
Hallertau	4 %	15 g	60 min
Hallertau	4 %	5 g	1 min

◀ If you're going Belgian and using spices like coriander, orange peel, or grains of paradise, add them during the last 5 minutes of the boil (see page 103).

④ CHILL

Target original gravity: 1.046

⑤ FERMENT

YEAST STRAIN	AMOUNT	TEMPERATURE	FERMENTATION
Hefeweizen Ale (WLP300)	⅓ tube	68°F	2 weeks
Target final gravity:			1.013

◀ Because the malts in wheat beers are so mild, this beer is ready to drink as soon as it's carbonated. No need to mellow your bottles for weeks in the fridge.

⑥ BOTTLE

Bottling sugar: 28 g

🧪 EXPERIMENT

Witbier: Add 5 oz Flaked Wheat and 2 oz Aromatic malt, then zest some citrus fruits into the boil for the last 5 minutes. Try tangerines, oranges, grapefruit, or just toss in a kumquat or two (see page 111). Switch to Belgianwit Ale yeast (WLP400) and a warmer fermentation.

Berliner Weisse: Add 14 g lactic acid at bottling, or mash with 2 oz Sour malt. See page 101.

Kristalweizen: Use a secondary fermenter and cold-condition it (39–46°F) in your beer fridge for a week. See LEARN TO LAGER, page 43.

Roggenbier: Replace the Wheat malt with 1 lb Rye malt. See page 102.

SAISON

Saison is a beer-maker's beer. Refreshing but complex, rustic but crisp, with a working man's provenance and a sophisticated taste, it's a wonder that saison is not more popular. In fact, even in its native Belgium, saisons were practically extinct by the end of the 19th century—until post–World War I enthusiasm for uniquely Belgian quirks brought the style back. Saisons were born centuries earlier, on Wallonian farms as a way to keep itinerant workers refreshed and hydrated, but sober enough to swing a scythe.

Saison means season, and—like its richer French cousin, the bière de garde—it was brewed in the winter and aged until summer. This was a peasant beer, made with whatever ingredients were on hand—old hops, surplus winter grains—and the aging process, plus the addition of spices, helped meld weird flavors, including the occasional bacteria contamination. Saisons are the original session beers and should be dry and smooth. But like any good Belgian beer, the yeast is always front and center with a unique peppery spiciness. Managing tricky Saison yeast strains (about as hard working as those boozy Walloons) can be the biggest challenge when making this style.

MALT Belgian Pilsner malt is the classic base. Historically, brewers would often toss in spelt, wheat, and other grains. You can get away with just Pilsner (Dupont's famous saison uses nothing but), or add a dash of Munich or Vienna malt for character. A little Wheat malt will help with head retention.

HOPS Saison is another good opportunity to use old hops. Earthy is best for this rustic brew: Stick with Hallertau, Fuggle, Kent Goldings or Styrian Goldings.

YEAST Saison yeast is unique in its ability to handle super-high temperatures (up to 90°F) without producing tons of esters. You'll get some of those fruity notes, but your saison should be nothing like a Belgian strong ale. If you can't find saison-specific yeast, use a Belgian yeast, or something as highly attenuating as you can—you want your finished beer to be as dry as possible. (It's rumored that Dupont uses a red wine yeast.)

ORIGINAL GRAVITY 1.050–1.065

STRENGTH 5–7% ABV

BEERS TO TRY Jolly Pumpkin Bam Bière, Ommegang Hennepin, Lost Abbey Red Barn, Pretty Things Jack D'Or, Odonata Saison, Ithaca Ground Break

1 MASH

GRAINS	AMOUNT (wt)
Belgian Pilsner malt	2 lb 4 oz
Wheat malt	4 oz
Vienna malt	2 oz

Bring 5 qt strike water to 156°F / Mash for 60 min at **146°F**

◀ Mashing at this lower temperature produces more fermentable sugars, which your yeast will happily destroy during fermentation, producing a dry, refreshing beer.

2 SPARGE

Target pre-boil gravity: **1.037**

3 BOIL

HOP VARIETY	ALPHA ACID	AMOUNT (g)	BOIL TIME
Hallertau	4 %	20 g	60 min
White table sugar	—	3 oz	15 min
Hallertau	4 %	10 g	1 min

◀ Adding sugar to the boil is another slightly counterintuitive way to ensure a drier final beer. Since table sugar is fully fermentable, it will contribute alcohol—but no flavor or sweetness—to your saison.

4 CHILL

Target original gravity: **1.059**

5 FERMENT

YEAST STRAIN	AMOUNT	TEMPERATURE	FERMENTATION
Belgian Saison II (WLP566)	½ tube	72°F	2 weeks

Target final gravity: **1.010**

◀ Saison yeasts can tolerate even higher temperatures, so this is a great beer to brew in the summer.

6 BOTTLE

Bottling sugar: **28 g**

🧪 EXPERIMENT

Brown (or Black) Saison: Add 2–8 oz Carafa malt to the mash.

Sour Saison: Add 14 g lactic acid at bottling, or mash with 2 oz Sour malt. *See page 101.*

Rustic Saison: Channel those old farmers and look beyond barley to round out your mash with rich, earthy notes: Add 1–6 oz spelt, buckwheat, or other grains. *See page 102.*

Monasteries had a rough run while Belgium changed hands again and again leading up to the 19th century. By the time the monasteries reopened for good in the 1830s, after Napoleon left town, Belgium's beer culture was a mess—far from the boozy Shangri-La it is today. Beers were weak and sour, and much cheaper to import than to make. During World War I things got even worse, but its end left Belgians craving local fare, and a Belgian beer tradition was invented.

Palm Speciale was an entry in a contest for "The Improvement of Belgian Beer." Duvel opened in 1923, using a British yeast. Orval opened in 1931, and Westmalle followed in 1933, releasing a tripel—the first of its kind—they called trappist. Today there are eight trappist breweries, and all but one (La Trappe, in the Netherlands) are in Belgium.

"Abbey beer" is a bit of a catchall category that includes Belgian strong golden and Belgian strong dark ales, as well as trappist ales. Brewed at monasteries, trappist beers often differ from their secular brothers in name and provenance only. They come in a range of styles, numbered according to their strength. Singels are rare, low-gravity versions, brewed for the monks and practically unknown outside the monasteries. Dubbels are strong and dark, with caramely, raisiny flavors from the malt, and some spiciness from the yeast. Tripels are paler, stronger, and crisper. Quadrupels are the imperial Abbey ales—as strong as you can handle but still deceptively smooth.

MALT Use mostly Belgian Pilsner malt. Singels take a couple of ounces of Aromatic or Special B malt; dubbels add to that 5 to 10 ounces of Munich malt; tripels replace the dark stuff with light sugar (2 to 6 ounces).

Adding sugar to the boil will boost the alcohol content without adding more proteins, so the beer will stay light and drinkable. This gives Abbey ales their hidden kick. Belgian brewers traditionally use different colors of caramelized sugar syrups, but homebrew stores will often stock so-called "Belgian light candi sugar." The little white crystals are basically table sugar (see page 109), so try something more exciting. We've even had an Abbey ale made with stevia (but we wouldn't recommend that).

HOPS Saaz and Styrian Goldings are the traditional Belgian hops.

YEAST Choose a Belgian strain, of course, and something strong enough to handle high-gravity fermentations if you're making a big tripel or a quad.

ORIGINAL GRAVITY 1.060–1085. Even higher for quads.

STRENGTH 6–9% ABV

BEERS TO TRY *Dark/Dubbel*: New Belgium Abbey Ale, Brooklyn Local 2, Lost Abbey Lost and Found. *Golden/Tripel*: Allagash Curieux, Russian River Damnation, Unibroue Fin du Monde. *Quadrupel*: Ommegang Three Philosophers, Avery Reverend, Lost Abbey Judgment Day, Green Flash Grand Cru

① MASH

GRAINS	AMOUNT (wt)
Belgian Pilsner malt	2 lb 8 oz
Munich malt	8 oz
Special B malt	4 oz
Aromatic malt	2 oz
Bring 6 qt strike water to 158°F / Mash for 60 min at	148°F

◀ This recipe will produce a dubbel. For a stronger, lighter-colored tripel, eliminate the Munich and Special B malts, and add 1 lb Pilsner malt (then adjust the boil as noted below).

② SPARGE   Target pre-boil gravity: 1.046

③ BOIL

HOP VARIETY	ALPHA ACID	AMOUNT (g)	BOIL TIME
Styrian Goldings	5 %	15 g	60 min
Belgian dark candi syrup	—	4 oz	15 min

◀ For a drier, crisper tripel, replace the Belgian dark candi syrup with white table sugar. Unlike dark candi syrup, table sugar ferments completely, leaving almost no taste behind.

④ CHILL   Target original gravity: 1.080

⑤ FERMENT

YEAST STRAIN	AMOUNT	TEMPERATURE	FERMENTATION
Abbey Ale (WLP530)	½ tube	70°F	2 weeks
	Target final gravity:		1.017

◀ A warmer fermentation draws out the Abbey ale yeast's distinctive fruity notes, which define this style.

⑥ BOTTLE   Bottling sugar: 22 g

🧪 EXPERIMENT

Special-Sugar Dubbel: Dark candi syrup is traditional, and imparts a lot of color, but try using dark cane sugars like demerara or turbinado instead. Molasses and dark maple syrups work great, too. Add 5 oz of any of these to your kettle—at the end of the boil, so you don't degrade their flavors. *See page 109.*

PILSNER

Unlike the creation stories of other beers, pilsner's comes date-stamped: November 11, 1842. That's the day Josef (some say Felix) Groll introduced the city of Pilsen to the beer that would become its namesake.

Pale ale was all the rage in England, and for years, Bohemian brewers were scrambling to imitate it—and coming up short each time. German brewers were after the pale, too, and they knew something the Czechs didn't: Lagering, or fermenting and aging beers at colder temperatures, produced a lighter product. Perfected in the northern city of Einbeck, where brewers made a uniquely clean, clear, cave-aged beer famous throughout Germany (even Martin Luther supposedly swigged it at Worms), lagering migrated south to Munich and spawned dozens of new styles: dunkels, bocks, doppelbocks, and dortmunders, but all of them dark and malty. German brewers couldn't crack the pale, despite sending spies to London breweries to steal samples in hollowed-out canes. That is, until a wandering monk slipped Groll a vial of German lager yeast, and the pilsner was born.

Flavorless yeast and Pilsen's naturally mineral-free water let the local delicate Moravian barley and spicy Saaz hops shine. Pilsner exploded at the 1873 Vienna World's Fair and soon became the most sought-after style on earth, but no one else could make it quite like Pilsen. American brewers, stuck with hard Great Lakes water and rich, 6-row barley lightened their beers with corn and rice, and still do today. Those mass-market brews have stigmatized the style, but don't let that stop you from making a pilsner worth stealing.

MALT It's totally possible to go entirely Pilsner malt on this one, though an ounce or two of slightly toasted malt like Vienna or Munich, or a light Crystal, can be an interesting touch. Two-row malt is fine, and will make mashing a little easier, but your beer won't be as light and clear.

HOPS Nothing but Saaz if you're going after Groll's original. German versions are lighter on the hops, but still noble: Tettnanger or Hallertau (Mt. Hood and Liberty are the U.S. versions).

YEAST There aren't nearly as many varieties of lager yeasts as ale yeasts, but you'll find a few variations. In general, if it's German, it'll make a slightly richer beer; Czech yeasts will be dry and crisp.

ORIGINAL GRAVITY Around 1.050.

STRENGTH 4.5–5.5% ABV

BEERS TO TRY *German*: Victory Prima Pils, Tröegs Sunshine Pils, Samuel Adams Noble Pils, Trumer Pils, North Coast Scrimshaw Pils. *Bohemian*: Lagunitas Pils, Moonlight Reality Czeck, Santa Cruz Mountain Brewery Pilsner. *Imperial*: Odell Double Pilsner.

① MASH

GRAINS	AMOUNT (wt)
Belgian Pilsner malt	2 lb 4 oz
Carapils malt	3 oz

Bring 5 qt strike water to 163°F / Mash for 60 min at	153°F

② SPARGE

Target pre-boil gravity: 1.034

Pilsen's famously soft water helped keep grain tannins in check and hops from getting too sharp (unlike those in sulfurous Burton-on-Trent's pale ales). Unless your tap water smells like eggs, you should be okay. If you're worried, add a few cups of distilled water to your mash.

③ BOIL

HOP VARIETY	ALPHA ACID	AMOUNT (g)	BOIL TIME
Saaz	3 %	30 g	60 min
Saaz	3 %	20 g	30 min
Saaz	3 %	15 g	15 min
Saaz	3 %	7 g	1 min

④ CHILL

Target original gravity: 1.054

⑤ FERMENT

YEAST STRAIN	AMOUNT	TEMPERATURE	FERMENTATION
Pilsner Lager (WLP800)	1 tube	55°F	4 weeks

Target final gravity: 1.014

Lager yeasts work cool, and they work slow. Primary fermentation will take a while—up to two weeks. Take hydrometer readings every couple of days, and when the gravity levels out, rack into a secondary fermenter for lagering. This takes even longer, so be patient! (See page 42.)

⑥ BOTTLE

Bottling sugar: 28 g

🧪 EXPERIMENT

Helles Bock: Replace the Carapils malt with Munich, for a richer malt flavor.

Dark Dunkel Bock: Add a few ounces of Chocolate or 120°L Crystal malt to the mash.

Kölsch: Use a German Ale yeast (WLP029) instead of a lager yeast and ferment warmer (around 62°F) before lagering to make a Kölsch, Cologne's classic session beer.

BARLEYWINE

There's nothing better to fight the stigma of British beer (weak, warm, and flat) than barleywine (strong, warm, and flat). That says something about British beer—what it lacks in refreshment, it makes up for in flavor.

In 19th-century Britain, the poor made do with cheap, dark-roasted malts and smoky beers; pale malts were reserved for gentry drinks, like IPAs. The palest of the pale—so-called "white malt"—was used to brew barleywines. Originally brewed on nobles' estates just after the October harvest, barleywines used the freshest malts and tons of just-picked Kent Goldings hops. Of course, all those fresh, earthy flavors changed radically when the beer was aged until the next harvest—and sometimes much longer. (Some lords would brew a batch to celebrate the birth of a son, and drink it when he turned 18.) The J.W. Lees barleywine is 100 percent Pale Ale malt, with no specialty grains at all, but you wouldn't know it. Aging smooths out the hops' bite and mellows the alcohol, giving barleywines the character of a much more complicated beer.

Some like an old barleywine with its notes of sherry and oak, but don't turn down one fresh from the fermenter. When they're young and super hoppy, barleywines can hold their own against the strongest imperial IPAs.

MALT Stick with Maris Otter or Pale Ale malt (a lot of it), and maybe add a little Crystal malt—but no more than 10 ounces. Use a low mash temperature to extract as much sugar from the mash as you can. This will pave the way for a more complete fermentation, and prevent your finished beer from turning out too sweet.

HOPS Use a lot of them. If you're a traditionalist, you can use only Kent Goldings. But when the beer is aged, the hop character will diminish, and after 6 months or so it won't matter what kind you used. High-alpha-acid hops like Chinook are a good bet for bittering, and if you're going to dry-hop, stick with the classics: Cascade or Kent Goldings.

YEAST Use a highly attenuative strain, like California Ale yeast. The key is to use enough of it. Pour in at least ¾ of a tube for primary fermentation. Because you'll be aging your barleywine for a long time before you bottle it, you'll need to add a small amount of yeast—about ⅛ of a tube—along with your priming sugar, at bottling time.

ORIGINAL GRAVITY 1.080–1.120

STRENGTH 8–12% ABV

BEERS TO TRY Sierra Nevada Bigfoot, Avery Hog Heaven, Green Flash Barleywine, Tröegs Flying Mouflan, Kuhnhenn's Bourbon Barrel Barleywine, AleSmith Old Numbskull, Stone Old Guardian

① MASH

GRAINS	AMOUNT (wt)
Maris Otter malt	4 lb 4 oz
Biscuit malt	4 oz
80°L Crystal malt	2 oz
Bring 10 qt strike water to 158°F / Mash for 60 min at	148°F

◀ This relatively simple recipe makes a beer meant to be aged. If you can't wait a few months, try adding some complexity with a few more ounces of specialty malts—like Chocolate, Caramunich, or Special B.

② SPARGE   Target pre-boil gravity: 1.065

◀ If your pre-boil gravity isn't within range, you can add sugar during the boil. Try 3 oz of brown sugar, added for the last 15 minutes of the boil. It will strengthen the beer—but will thin the body out a bit, too.

③ BOIL

HOP VARIETY	ALPHA ACID	AMOUNT (g)	BOIL TIME
Chinook	11.5 %	20 g	60 min
Columbus	12 %	15 g	20 min
Cascade	6 %	10 g	1 min

④ CHILL   Target original gravity: 1.105

⑤ FERMENT

YEAST STRAIN	AMOUNT	TEMPERATURE	FERMENTATION
California Ale (WLP001)	¾ tube	68°F	4 weeks

Target final gravity: 1.025

◀ This beer is very strong, and the yeast might take a while to ferment all of its sugars. Some breweries rouse the yeast by taking the fermenters (barrels, in their case) for a roll around the brewery. If you notice your gravity has stopped decreasing, but is still far from the target, shake your fermenter a bit. When you hit the target gravity—it might take up to 4 weeks—make sure to transfer your beer to a secondary fermenter and age it for at least 6 months to 1 year, then add ⅛ tube of yeast when you bottle.

⑥ BOTTLE   Bottling sugar: 17 g

🧪 EXPERIMENT

Barrel-Aged Barleywine: Add 1½ oz wood chips, liquor-soaked if you want, to your beer in the secondary fermenter. *See page 112.*

Old Ale: Add 2 oz Chocolate malt, and replace all hop additions with milder Fuggle hops.

Old Wild: Add ¼ tube brettanomyces (wild yeast) to a secondary fermenter. *See page 115.*

GREG KOCH

COFOUNDER AND CEO, STONE BREWING CO.

You started Stone in 1996, right in the midst of a craft beer recession.
The industry was growing 25 percent every year. Then in '96 it was 7 percent and in '97, 2 percent. The bubble had burst, but we didn't know it, we were so focused on making beer. I'd talk to bars and wholesalers, and they'd pat me on the head and say, Sorry son, the micro-beer craze is over. It's imports now. And I'd say, Stone isn't a micro beer. Stone is Stone. We're going to brew beers we like. I had the sense to realize that this is a good business model.

These days, you're not alone—in fact, you guys often collaborate with other craft breweries.
Collaborating lets us make beers we might not have had an idea for ourselves. It's like a jam session with other musicians. They bring their styles, and you go in different directions, tossing ideas back and forth. Or a brewer comes in with an idea and we say, We love that song, let's play it together.

We love your gargoyle logo. Where did that idea come from?
It started with our first beer, Stone Pale Ale. The gargoyle is the same today as it was then. It was an effort to show our difference. I know that's a little marketing-speaky, but stronger, more unique beers need stronger imagery. It's a beacon, or it could be a warning.

Is that the same idea behind Arrogant Bastard, and the "You're Not Worthy" rant on the bottle?
That was a recipe we developed while homebrewing other beers. We knew only a few of our friends could ever choke it down, but they would love it, so I got really antisocial with the label. I did my best to warn people away. But it's frustrating when we're painted with this broad brush as, well, arrogant bastards. Really, it's about being, and celebrating, better. It's a line in the sand. We're not going to cross it to come to your side, but we invite you to come to our side. This is where the great stuff is. This is where it's at!

ESCONDIDO, CALIFORNIA
EST. 1996
SIZE: 120,000 barrels/year
OUR FAVORITES: Sublimely Self-Righteous Ale, Arrogant Bastard Ale, Imperial Russian Stout

Stone beers can come on a little strong. Greg Koch and Steve Wagner's Southern California brewery makes powerful IPAs, rich smoky porters, and an impossibly dark Russian stout they release, as a challenge, in the heat of the summer. The names don't help: Ruination, Arrogant Bastard, Sublimely Self-Righteous. But stop by the brewery itself, and (through the heavy castle doors) it's a leafy green oasis of local flora, organic eats, and tap after tap of beer from Stone and their far-flung network of brewing friends. This is Stone's generous side—founded in a recession, but ranked the best brewery in the world four years later, Stone has had a dizzying ride, and they work hard to share life at the top. The brewery feels welcoming and calm, and then, almost, a friendly prank, when the rug is pulled out and your comfort zone succumbs to another mind-bending beer.

Specialty Grains

THE BACKSTORY

Drinks like bourbon have strict rules about what grains can and can't go into the mash tun. Beer, lucky for you, is wide open. True, grains like corn and rice get a bad rap in the U.S. But blame the large-scale producers who use them to water beer down, not give it new flavors. Craft brewers can make a mean rice beer, corn beer was a Colonial favorite, and rye is as traditional as barley in places like Russia and Scandinavia. Even small twists like using dark grains in unexpected places can give your homebrew a whole new angle. And then, of course, there's just good old American excess: using more, more, more to make big, powerful beers.

EXTRA GRAINS

Want to go big? Er, we mean, "imperial"? The name just means "strong," a hold-over from the days when Brits would send their biggest beers to the Russian Empire—the czars liked heavier stuff—but now imperial IPAs, imperial stouts, even imperial pilsners are edging out their svelter brethren for tap space.

Any beer can get a boost by using more grains. The basic idea is to make a bigger mash to get more wort, and then boil it longer than normal to make a super-concentrated 1-gallon batch. Think 4 to 5 pounds of base malt and an extra couple ounces of any flavoring malts (adjust your mash water volume accordingly). Of course, to balance all that malt, you'll need more hops, especially on the bittering side. An ounce or more for bittering alone wouldn't be outrageous. You'll want to use twice as much yeast, too (half a tube at least), and rack to a secondary fermenter (see page 42) to age and mellow the strong flavors.

DARK MALTS

Adding dark malts to light beers is a great way to shake up an old style. We like using Weyermann's Carafa malts, which come de-husked, so they have all the color and flavor but none of the bitter tannins of Roasted Barley. Mid-range roasted malts like Chocolate, dark Crystal, or Munich work well, too. Adding 3 to 10 ounces of Carafa to a pale ale recipe will make what some West Coast brewers call a Cascadian dark ale. Try some in a wheat beer for a take on a dunkelweizen or an even darker weizenbock. Why stop there? Even saisons can handle a little color.

SMOKED MALT

Before coal-fired kilns, grains were dried over wood, and the beer they made was rich and smoky. If liquid bacon sounds delicious, you can buy Smoked malt in one of two varieties: PEATED MALT (also called distiller's malt), which is smoked over peat; and RAUCHMALT, which is smoked over beechwood.

If you have a grill, you can make your own smoked malt. Light a small handful of briquettes, and cover them with wet wood chips. Here's where you experiment: Try birch, cherry, maple, mesquite—whatever! Fill a shallow basket (like a colander) with unmilled Pale Ale malt, set it on a rack over the coals, cover the grill, open the vents, and cook for about an hour. Be sure to let your home-smoked grains mellow out for about 2 weeks before using them. Fresh from the grill, they'll be overwhelmingly smoky.

ROAST YOUR OWN

Twenty years ago, grains like Brown malt were a rare find in homebrew shops. Not so today, but roasting your own grains can help you dial in specific flavors that can be hard to replicate by mixing and matching pre-toasted malt. Plus, it makes your kitchen smell great.

Start with unmilled Pale Ale malt. Spread the grains out on a cookie sheet and, if you want, sprinkle them with water for a more caramelized flavor. Roast at 350°F for anywhere from 15 minutes to an hour, depending on how dark you want the malt to be. A half hour will give you toasted, amber malt or Grape-Nuts flavor; an hour gets you the darker roast of Brown malt. Take it out of the oven and spritz with water to stop the roast. Like home-smoked malt, let it rest for 2 weeks.

SOUR MALT

Also called Acidulated malt or, in German, Sauermalz, Sour malt is regular, 2-row barley that has been dosed with a small amount of lactic acid. Use 1 to 2 ounces in a wheat beer to make a sour Berliner weisse. That amount in a stout will give it the slight tang of a Guinness.

GRAINS BEYOND BARLEY

We'll be honest: There's a reason brewers stick to barley. Beers made entirely from other grains are usually terrible—thin and flavorless. That said, a touch of any of them (1 to 10 ounces, say) can change the flavor and body of your beer in ways plain old barley can't. So experiment, but use sparingly.

Remember that these specialty grains most likely will not be available malted. That means that if you're using a lot of them (say, 1/3 of your mash or more), you might want to cook them yourself first to unlock their starches. It's called "gelatinization." That way, the extra enzymes in your base malt can convert those new starches, too. It's not totally necessary, but it's easy—just boil the grains in a quart of water for 15 to 30 minutes (until they soften), let the mixture cool for about 5 minutes, then add it straight to your mash just after you stir in the malted barley. If the grain is flaked, torrified, or otherwise processed, you can get away with adding it to your mash raw.

Your real concern will be a sticky mash—be sure to add some rice hulls to help it drain more easily. Available at any homebrew shop, these crunchy, fibrous husks are flavorless, but make your mash loose and porous.

BEERS TO TRY *Dark malt*: Deschutes Hop in the Dark, Stone Sublimely Self-Righteous, Jolly Pumpkin Bam Noire. *Smoked malt*: Alaskan Smoked Porter, Stone Smoked Porter, Weyerbacher Fireside. *Beyond barley*: Founders Rye-PA, Great Divide Samurai, Rogue Morimoto Soba Ale, Anderson Valley Oatmeal Stout, Left Hand Rye Bock, Sixpoint Righteous Rye.

Taylor Rees
Head Brewer
GREAT DIVIDE

Denver's Great Divide wanted a light, sessionable beer—something to balance their big guns like the aptly named Yeti, Titan, and Claymore—but with every brewery from Colorado to Connecticut releasing summer wits and weizens, Great Divide thought the world had enough wheat beers. So they used rice. A lot of it. And, surprisingly, it works. Samurai uses less rice than Budweiser (only 10 to 15 percent), but doesn't try to hide the grain's natural flavors: creamy, mild, delicately fruity. Their Hoss lager has a big kick of rye spice; even Collette, their saison, has some rice in it. Weird grains don't scare Great Divide, and they shouldn't scare you.

"**We use flaked brown rice.** The flaking process gelatinizes it, so you need enzymes from malt, but you don't need to boil the rice first. If you were to use plain old rice, you'd want to crack it open and boil it beforehand."

"**If you were to use tons of adjuncts,** you might have too many simple sugars in your wort when you first pitch the yeast, and the cells might skip the reproduction phase and just start eating. In that case, you'd want to pitch heavier."

"**Keep in mind that rye, like wheat, has no husk, so draining your mash is hard.** Rice hulls help, but count on a long process. We once made a 50 percent rye roggenbier on our 10-gallon pilot setup. I have no idea how we'd do it on our full system, but as a homebrewer, it's definitely possible."

GRAINS TO TRY

BUCKWHEAT	1–6 oz

Buckwheat is earthy and a little oily. It can occasionally smell a little funky, because it contains capric and capryllic acids—the same stuff produced by wild bacteria in some sour beers.

CORN	3–6 oz

Corn or maize can either be ground into grits or flaked. Both types lighten body and give beer a slightly gritty, almost meaty flavor. Grits made from Indian corn will be much more interesting.

OATS	3–6 oz

Oats have lots of protein, fat, and oil that will destroy foam, so don't use too much. A dash gives stouts a smooth, rich finish. Toasted in your oven at 400°F for 10 minutes, they'll give a great cookie-dough aroma. (Be sure to let them mellow for 2 weeks before using.)

RICE	1–6 oz

Rice is even drier than corn, and, if you're using American rice, has zero flavor. Brown, basmati, and jasmine are more interesting, and wild rice, though not technically a rice at all (and pretty pricey), has a nutty flavor that's truly unique.

RYE	No more than 10 oz

Rye has a nice crisp spiciness, but turns mushy in the mash. Roggenbier is a German beer made with tons of rye—sometimes more than half—and it's one of the few delicious exceptions to our mostly barley rule.

SPELT	1–6 oz

Spelt is nutty and very thick. Your mash will be sticky, and your beer will probably be a little cloudy.

UNMALTED BARLEY	2–3 oz

Minimal flavor. Because of its extra protein, Guinness uses it for their foam.

UNMALTED WHEAT	3–6 oz

Lots of protein, so it'll give your beer a better head and a thick, milkshake-like body, depending on how much you use.

Spices & Herbs

THE BACKSTORY

When hops burst onto the brewing scene in the 1500s, brewers gave up a thousands-of-years-old tradition of spicing beers with a greenhouse full of wild, medicinal, and narcotic plants. Today, spiced beers are mainly confined to the holiday-ale or summer-witbier shelves, and ruled by the Belgian brewing mantra that if you can pick out any one spice, the brewer used too much of it. But don't let that stop you. A dash of spice can make almost any beer tantalizingly complex; a little more and you're crossing into territory unexplored for the past 500 years—except, of course, by homebrewers like you.

BASIC SPICING TECHNIQUES

Before you add spice to a beer, adjust the recipe by using a tad less hops. You won't want their stronger flavors to overpower your spices.

In general, you'll want to use between 2 and 10 grams of each herb for a moderately spiced brew. If you're going for intense flavor, bump up the quantity.

Add the spices to your kettle at the very end of the boil, for just a minute or so. You're treating them delicately, like your aroma hop addition. Don't worry about using a mesh bag to hold your spices—you'll strain them out when you pour the wort into your fermenter.

For a slightly more delicate flavor, spice your beer by putting the spices into your hopback (see page 106).

Look for fresh herbs when possible. Basil, ginger, lavender, mint, and kaffir lime are easy enough to find at the grocery store. When you use fresh herbs, it's best not to boil them. Instead, put them in the hopback, or use them in a tea.

Make a tea by steeping your spice mixture in hot water for a few minutes and straining the spices out. Add the (chilled) tea to the beer at bottling time, or in a secondary fermenter. How much to use is up to you—pull out a small sample of beer, and add a few drops to see what it tastes like, then scale that up to a full-gallon batch.

HOLIDAY ALE

While the brewers of some of our favorite holiday beers keep their exact spice mixtures a secret, the basics aren't hard to guess: ginger, cinnamon, anise, allspice, and cloves (think gingerbread). Start with a total of 2 grams (or about 1 teaspoon) of spices.

JUNIPER ALE

Juniper-flavored beers, called sahti, are traditional in Finland. There, brewers sparge grain through a filter bed of juniper and alder branches, and sometimes add juniper sap to the wort as well. You can recreate this in a hopback. Fill it with juniper twigs and berries, then pour your wort through.

SUGGESTIONS

- Anise
- Basil
- Birch bark
- Cardamom
- Chicory
- Chili peppers
- Cinnamon
- Cloves
- Cocoa powder
- Coconut
- Coriander
- Fennel
- Fenugreek
- Galangal
- Ginger
- Grains of paradise
- Heather tips
- Kaffir lime
- Juniper berries
- Lavender
- Lemongrass
- Licorice root
- Mint
- Nutmeg
- Pepper
- Rosemary
- Saffron
- Sage
- Spruce tips
- Saint-John's-wort
- Valerian
- Vanilla bean

GRUIT ALE

To make something similar to the ale that 14th-century Europeans drank, boil a wort with 2 grams of bog myrtle (also known as myrica gale or sweet gale), 2 grams of wild rosemary (or marsh rosemary or Labrador tea), and 2 grams of yarrow. (Look for these at your local hippie herb shop.) Then dry-hop with 2 grams of each in your fermenter—alcohol will pull out even more of their resins. These herbs can be mildly narcotic, so be careful!

HEATHER ALE

The Picts, a Celtish tribe in the British Isles, were famous for their heather beer. Heather tips are delicious—floral and piney—and they make a great substitute for hops. (Any homebrew shop will have them.) To make your own heather ale, boil your wort with 1½ cups of heather tips for 60 minutes. Then use a hopback filled with ½ cup heather. (Yes, we know, this seems like a lot of heather—but trust us, it tastes like no beer you've ever had, and is definitely worth a try.)

HOT PEPPERS

Dried or fresh chili peppers can be added at the end of the boil, like a spice, or steeped in the secondary fermenter for a few days, like fruit. Roasting them in your oven before steeping gives off a great, smoky flavor. As little as 7 grams will give you some definite heat, but it also depends on what kind of pepper you use. If you're going with fresh ones, we'd take the seeds out first.

COFFEE

Start with 20 grams and go up from there. Grind the beans coarsely, and pour your wort through them on its way into the fermenter—or soak them in your fermenting beer, like dry-hopping, and let alcohol strip out the beans' oils. The key is never to boil your beans.

CHOCOLATE

Solid chunks of chocolate need to be boiled a bit to dissolve them in your wort. Start with an 80-gram piece. A regular old chocolate bar will have cocoa butter in it, which will inhibit a good head on your finished beer. Cocoa powder is butter-free, but subtler. Use more, and add at the very end of the boil.

NUTS

Yes, we know: not a spice! Well, nuts don't add any fermentable sugars to your beer—only flavor—so we're treating them as another aromatic herb. Add at least ¼ cup ground-up, roasted nuts—like walnuts, pecans, or chestnuts—straight into the mash. If you choose to roast your own, just be sure to let them age for a week.

BEERS TO TRY *Herbs*: O'So Picnic Ants (pepper), The Bruery Trade Winds Tripel (basil). *Juniper Ales*: Rogue Juniper Ale, Dogfish Head Sah-tea. *Holiday Ales*: Great Lakes Christmas, Anchor Christmas, Harpoon Winter Warmer, Berkshire Brewing Co. Cabin Fever Ale. *Hot peppers*: Rogue Chipotle Ale, Left Brain Devil's Thumb, Red Eye Cart Ride to Mexico, Dogfish Head Theobroma (chilies and Aztec cocoa). *Coffee*: Sixpoint Gorilla Warfare, Tröegs Java Head, AleSmith Speedway Stout. *Chocolate*: Brooklyn Black Chocolate Stout, Rogue Mocha Porter.

John Trogner
Founder
TRÖEGS

At first, John and his brother Chris thought Tröegs would be a brewpub, but they were always too busy making beer to think about cooking. Still, their foodie dreams creep into the brew kettle: Their Christmas ale is made with sour cherries and local honey, a stout is infused with gourmet cacao nibs, and then there's our favorite, Java Head, packed with flavor from the best Kenyan beans. John, who likes roasting his morning cup himself, explained the tricks to a great coffee beer.

"**At first, we tried tossing ground beans into the boil,** but not only was it a total mess, it was really acrid and bitter, too. Then we had the French press idea: Put the ground beans in the hopback, steep wort in it for a few minutes, and run it through."

"**The type of beans you use really matters.** We wanted to match the beans with the hops and the malt. Colombian beans were way too acidic. We chose Kenyan because they're citrusy and a little nutty, and also have a lot of cocoa flavor if they're roasted right. It's almost like a stout character already."

"**You don't want them too oily**—if you can see an oil slick on the beans, there's too much. And use a very coarse grind, so there's less surface area to extract the oils."

"**Dry-hopping with coffee would be great.** We were going to try it, but on a 100-barrel brew, it's a huge pain in the ass. Only a homebrewer could do it."

Extra Hops

THE BACKSTORY

For such a delicate and flavorful plant, hops get treated pretty rough. Brewers worship those cones, then chuck them into wort and boil them like hell. Boiling makes beer bitter, but it also ruins a lot of the precious oils in hops that make beer taste great. Be nice to your hops with techniques that minimize boil time and maximize oil extraction, and they'll open up flavors you never knew beer could have.

FIRST-WORT HOPPING

Add a third of your finishing aroma hops to your wort as soon as you remove the grains, and let them steep as you bring the wort to a boil. This works better the longer they steep. Like dry-hopping, this is a way to get at volatile hop oils that get destroyed by boiling.

LATE-HOPPING

Sierra Nevada flavors its famously citrusy beers by loading them with hops right at the end of the boil in a technique called late-hopping. By eliminating the traditional bittering addition, you'll preserve your beer's malt notes while still getting a ton of hop flavors. It will still taste bitter, but not sharp or biting. Try adding all the hops a recipe calls for within the final 10 minutes of your boil. Aroma hops, of course, are best for this.

HOPBACK

A hopback is a strainer filled with hops through which you filter your beer on its way into the fermenter. It'll give your beer an extra kick of aroma, plus it helps filter out some trub. (This technique works great for spices, too—see page 104 for some ideas.) Start with 7 grams. We like whole hops for this—pellets make the beer too cloudy.

DRY-HOPPING

Since any boiling at all deteriorates hops' aromatic oils, adding them to your beer once it's in the fermenter is a great way to get powerful hop flavors. Active yeast can strip out some hop character, so add them during a secondary fermentation (see page 42). Don't worry about sanitizing them—hops are naturally antiseptic, plus the beer you add them to will be acidic enough to keep infections at bay. As for which hops to use, you want them oily, like Centennial, Columbus, or Horizon. Try 15 to 30 grams per gallon—either whole or pellet.

GROW YOUR OWN HOPS

In the U.S., as in most hop-growing countries, hops are cultivated from rhizomes, or root cuttings, not seeds. When the female hop plant produces seeds, it does so at the expense of hop cones, so farmers ignore male-female fertilization altogether, and grow the plants straight from roots. Rhizomes are usually available at online stores from March to June. Plant your cutting early in the spring (March or April) in well-fertilized soil and, as it begins to grow, trim back all but the strongest 3 or 4 shoots (called bines). When the bines get long enough, wrap them around a couple long pieces of twine or a trellis—they'll grow fast, up to a foot a day in peak season. Pick the cones in August or September, when they just start to turn greenish-yellow. Let the cones air-dry, or pile them on a cookie sheet and put them in an oven at very low heat (130°F or so) for a few hours.

WET-HOPPING

If you do grow your own hop vines, you should really use your cones fresh from the plant. A few West Coast brewers do this. Both Sierra Nevada (see page 22) and Rogue (see page 70) brew so-called "wet-hopped" beers that are outrageously flavorful and overflowing with grassy hop aromas. When using fresh hops, stick to very late additions to the boil, or dry-hop, adding them to your secondary fermenter. Using 15 to 30 grams per gallon is a good start.

BEERS TO TRY *Wet-hopped*: Deschutes Hop Trip, Rogue Chatoe Rogue Wet Hop, Sierra Nevada Harvest series, Moonlight Homegrown, Port Brewing High Tide, Founders Harvest.

Jeremy Marshall
Head Brewer
LAGUNITAS

Northern California's Lagunitas hops beer like no one else. First, they dry-hop a lot—even their summer wheat beer, Little Sumpin' Sumpin', gets a dose. Then there's Jeremy's hop cannon: Built from the pressure chamber of an old cryogenic freezer, it fires a 70 psi stream of hop pellets straight into the fermenters. Jeremy reckons the pellets fly so fast they're on fire when they hit the beer. Don't have your own cannon? Try these tips from Jeremy instead:

"**People say to use aroma hops, but we use high-alpha hops instead.** I like the 'C' hops: Chinook, Centennial, Citra, and Columbus."

"**We use pellets because they fit in the cannon, and they dissolve in the beer.** If your pellets are hard and shiny, they haven't been milled right and will take a lot longer to dissolve. Same thing if they're huge."

"**After 24 hours of dry-hopping, the beer actually tastes worse—very planty—but don't worry.** After 3 days, the oils start to come out. Four days is about right—not much happens after that."

"**Always start with a freshly opened pouch of hops.** There's nothing worse than cheesy beer."

Sugars

THE BACKSTORY

If you mash them carefully, the right grains will give you all the sugars you need to make beer. Still, brewers have been augmenting that maltose with other sugars for ages, from Brits using East Indian molasses to Colonial Americans making do with pumpkins and potatoes. A little extra sugar will boost your beer's ABV, and can add flavors like maple, caramel, or butterscotch, while keeping your beer light and drinkable, since sugar won't add any extra proteins.

BASIC USE

When brewing with extra sugars, make sure that about three-quarters of what goes into your beer is grain, otherwise it'll taste cidery. Start with 5 ounces, and work your way up from there. You can add sugars either to the boil or to the fermenter. As with hops, spices, and fruits, the later in the brewing process you add sugar, the more flavor it will impart. If you're adding sugar to your fermenter, first boil it briefly in a little water to sanitize it. Let it cool, then add it to your fermenter once your yeast has started working. If you add it just after pitching, you'll overwhelm the yeast with a too-sugary beer.

Experimental sugars add lots of flavor when used for bottling, but they can be slow to carbonate your beer because they're more complex than plain ol' corn sugar. Boil, cool, and stir in ¼ cup of honey, molasses, or maple syrup, or 25 grams of brown or other cane sugar.

HONEY

You can replace half a beer's grain bill with honey (about 2 pounds) to make a drink called braggot. Make a wort as usual, adding the honey at the end of the boil to sanitize it without degrading its flavors. Make an all-honey mead by boiling 3 pounds honey in 1 gallon water for a minute or so, then fermenting it. Honey is almost half fructose, which is much harder than other sugars for yeast to eat. It might take a month or more for your braggot or mead to ferment fully and clear. Bring the big guns with a super-strong Champagne yeast and a teaspoon of yeast nutrient.

PUMPKIN

Pumpkins have been a part of American brewing since the first colonist ran out of British beer and decided to make his own. It's too bad these days the humble gourd is relegated to over-spiced novelty brews with jack-o'-lanterns on the label. You can do better. Pumpkins should be treated more like a sugar than a flavor addition. Split a small pumpkin in half and roast in a 325°F oven until it's juicy and caramelized. Scoop out the pulp and add it to your mash. (Sweet potatoes work, too, and don't need to be precooked.)

BEERS TO TRY Brooklyn Buzz Bomb (honey), Kuhnhenn Mayhem (caramelized beet sugar), Lagunitas Brown Shugga (just what it sounds like). *Pumpkin*: Southern Tier PumKing, Smuttynose Pumpkin. *Sweet potato*: Fullsteam Carver

AGAVE

Usually fermented to make tequila, but now a popular sweetener in hipster coffee shops. Slightly floral, like a more delicate honey.

BROWN SUGAR

White table sugar with a little molasses added to it. For a more prominent flavor, use molasses instead.

CANDI SUGAR

Pure sucrose, which is a highly fermentable sugar. This means that candi sugar—unless it's dark—won't add much flavor to your beer. It's only a step away from plain ol' table sugar.

CANDY

It's possible to use Jolly Ranchers and the like, either in the boil or as flavored bottling sugar. Crystallized ginger won't add much fermentable sugar, but tastes great. Chop up half an ounce and add it to the end of the boil.

CORN SUGAR

Not much flavor. Good for priming bottles.

DARK CANDI SYRUP

Adds lots of color and is popular with Belgian brewers (dark syrups give Flanders sours their hue). They oxidize fast, though, so beers made with syrup are best drunk fresh.

DEMERARA

Cane sugar with slight caramel notes. Turbinado is the same thing, just with more molasses.

HONEY

Full of dozens of different sugars and flavors, its effect on your beer depends on what kind of honey you use: clover, orange blossom, etc. Don't add it to the kettle—boiling honey too much will ruin its flavor.

JAGGERY

Indian palm sugar that's light and creamy, like maple syrup. Also called gur or kaong.

LACTOSE

Unfermentable milk sugar. Will add a Hershey-bar tang to your beer. It's great in stouts. Boil it to dissolve, and add it to the fermenter, or even the finished beer, since it's just for flavor—it won't ferment.

MAPLE SYRUP

Because of the water content in maple syrup, you'll need to use more of it than other sugars to really taste it in your beer. It's expensive, but if you're willing to pay, you can use up to 3 or 4 cups per batch.

MOLASSES (LIGHT, DARK, OR BLACKSTRAP)

Very strong, but makes for a rich, delicious, and dark beer. Use sparingly—¼ cup or so.

WHITE TABLE SUGAR

Made from beets or sugarcane. Flavorless at best, and sharp and cidery at worst. With so many other options, why bother with this one?

Fruits

THE BACKSTORY

Fruit beers trace back to the Egyptians, who used dates and pomegranates in their beer—but those sweet, cherry-spiked lambics are, more or less, a 20th-century invention. The big guys use fruit extracts or syrups (because they're cheaper and easier to handle on such a large scale); on your stove top, you can use the real deal. Most fruit beers out there are wheat beers—but that doesn't mean you can't make an awesome raspberry porter or pumpkin stout.

BASIC USE

The best way to use whole, fresh fruit is to add it to your beer in a secondary fermenter (see page 42). Use about a pound of fruit per gallon of beer. The alcohol will help strip out the fruit's oils, and the beer will be acidic enough that any wild yeast hidden in the fruit skins probably won't be able to get a foothold. There will be enough active yeast left in your wort to munch on the fruit's sugars and create more alcohol and carbon dioxide, so be sure you have enough headspace in your fermenter that no fruit pieces will pop up and get stuck in the airlock. Thawed frozen fruit is fine, too—and even easier, since it's already crushed.

Fruit concentrates and fruit syrups are fine additions as well, but can be very sugary (artificially sweetened), so be sure to add them during primary fermentation instead, while the beer is actively fermenting, or else they could build up too much pressure.

Fruit extracts, on the other hand, have no sugars, which means you can add an ounce or so to your fully fermented beer (along with the necessary priming sugar) when bottling.

Some homebrewers steep whole fruit in their wort for 15 to 30 minutes while it's chilling. This imparts a little fruit flavor while pasteurizing the fruit to kill any bugs that are hitching rides on its skin. You can strain out the fruit when you pour the wort into your fermenter—or not. It won't add a ton of flavor during primary fermentation, so there's no real benefit to leaving it in.

Unless it has been frozen or pasteurized in hot wort or boiling water before you add it to the fermenter, your fruit will have a little wild yeast in it, and there's always the chance that a few cells survive the acidity of the beer and start a new, funky fermentation. When you're brewing with fruit, know that your beer might end up a little sour. That's okay! Traditional fruit beers have a little tang to them. Those extra-sweet cherry beers girls are supposed to like are made with sugary syrups and then pasteurized to kill wild yeast and preserve the sugar. You're doing things the old-fashioned way.

FRUITS TO TRY

Brewing with fruit is trial-and-error. Some fruits will work wonderfully; others won't do much at all. Apricots, raspberries, cherries, and blackberries are all strongly flavored, and work well. (Traditional kriek producers throw the cherries—pits and all—into the secondary fermenter, where the pits give the beer an almondy bitterness.) Strawberries, peaches, mangoes, and blueberries are subtler—use 2 pounds per gallon, at least. We've heard jams are an effective work-around in a pinch, but they might make the finished product a bit cloudy, due to all the additional pectin.

USING CITRUS

Citrus fruits are a little different—all the flavorful oils you want are found in the peel. Carefully zest or grate the fruit, avoiding the bitter white pith. You'll only need a portion of one peel per batch. Try ¼ to ½ of a standard orange rind. Add the zest at the end of the boil, along with (or instead of) your aroma hops.

USING DRIED FRUIT

Some fruits are commonly dried (currants, say) and others just taste better that way (raisins are much more flavorful than grapes). Before you boil, scoop out 1 cup of wort and puree in it 2 ounces of dried fruit, then add the mixture back to your wort 10 minutes before the end of the boil.

BEERS TO TRY Dogfish Head Aprihop, Fullsteam Persimmon, Kuhnhenn Strawberry Panty Dropper, 21st Amendment Watermelon Wheat, Mountain Sun Blackberry Wheat.

SUGGESTIONS

FRESH FRUITS
Apricots
Blackberries
Blueberries
Cherries (sweet or sour)
Grapes
Mangoes
Nectarines
Passionfruit
Peaches
Plums
Raspberries
Strawberries
Watermelons

CITRUS FRUITS
Blood oranges
Grapefruit
Kumquats
Lemons
Limes
Oranges
Tangerines

DRIED FRUITS
Dried cranberries
Dates
Prunes
Raisins

Barrel-Aging

THE BACKSTORY

Barrel-aging means taking risks and being patient. Often, brewers age in old liquor barrels, but even fresh wood is full of flavor—as well as a host of funky micro-organisms—that will slowly instill your beer with the kind of deep, complex character of wines and whiskeys. The thing is, once your beer is in a barrel, or in a secondary fermenter filled with chips, you're brewing on the wood's terms. Sometimes your beer will taste awful for months—until one day it tastes perfect. Sometimes a wild infection can be lucky. No matter what, your beer will come off the wood completely changed from when it went in. If nothing else, it's exciting.

WHAT WOOD?

Budweiser is famously "beechwood aged," which, even according to Budweiser, just gives the yeast more surface area to act on, nothing more. Smell a handful of beechwood chips and you'll see what we mean. For real woody flavor, stick with oak. Oak wood contains a couple of flavor compounds brewers love: vanillin and tannin. French oak is sharper (more tannins) than American oak, which has more vanillin.

RAW WOOD CHIPS

Adding chips to your fermenter is much easier than finding a gallon-sized barrel, and you have more options in how you use them. Maximum contact with your beer will get maximum results, but wood, of course, floats. So stuff a small handful of chips in a mesh bag, along with a couple of marbles, boil the whole thing to sanitize it, and sink it in your beer. Use a secondary fermenter, since you'll be letting the beer sit for a while. Taste it every couple of weeks, and bottle when you feel it's ready. It's easiest to use a bucket as a fermenter for this, but make sure it's as oxygen-sealed as possible.

LIQUORED CHIPS

Now let's get those chips liquored up. Professional brewers have to account for every drop of alcohol in their beer—and it all has to get there through fermentation alone. So they wash out the liquor from every barrel they use (of course, some remains in the wood, but the ATF doesn't know that). You, on the other hand, don't account to nobody. Which means you can take a major shortcut: Age your beer on clean chips for the oak flavor, then, when you bottle it, add a few ounces of your booze of choice for the liquor flavor. It's less glamorous than a bourbon-soaked barrel, but it works.

Or, toss a couple of oak chips in a bottle of bourbon and let them sit for a few weeks to a few months (to a few years). Strain out the chips, and you'll have oaky bourbon and bourbony oak. (Char the chips with a torch before you soak them to amp up their oakiness.) Then add to a secondary fermenter.

BARRELS

This can be daunting. Barrels can cost hundreds of dollars and are usually enormous (30 gallons or more). Some homebrew shops sell smaller barrels, in the 2- to 5-gallon range. If you go this route, be warned: Those fresh barrels are exploding with oak flavor and will turn the first few batches you put in them into liquid lumber. A few micro-distilleries, like Tuthilltown, sell their used barrels, which will have a mellower flavor, plus some bourbon or rum character. They might look terrible, but don't worry—they'll swell when wet, and seal tight. If you use a barrel, like it or not, you're using wild yeast, too. The wood will already have bacterial critters living in it by the time you fill it with beer. They will change the beer's character for sure, but there won't be enough to ferment a batch on their own. So ferment your beer as usual, then transfer it into a barrel to age. If you want to ferment in a barrel, you'll have to add more wild yeast. Traditional lambic brewers bring bacteria to the barrel in the wort, which they leave out overnight to become infected. Flanders red brewers inoculate their barrels with a little old wort from another barrel. You can pour in a little brettanomyces or a lambic culture (see pages 114–115), or even empty in the dregs of a bottle of lambic or Flanders red and hope the bacteria takes up residence. Either way, you're now entering territory mysterious even to many professional brewers. There's still a lot we don't know about wild yeast, except that it takes a long time, and rarely works as you expect. Be patient, and good luck!

BEERS TO TRY Founders Kentucky and Canadian Breakfast Stouts, Great Divide Wood Chip IPA, The Bruery Black Tuesday, Avery Barrel-Aged Series.

Andy Parker
Senior Brewer and Barrel Wrangler
AVERY BREWING

Andy started Avery's barrel program 6 years ago with a dozen West Coast wine barrels and crossed fingers. They've had some bad luck along the way: A stout aged in rum barrels tasted great going into bottles, but was contaminated 4 weeks later. No one knows how it happened. But some infections, Andy learned, can be good. A strange mutant form of pediococcus bacteria took root in one of the barrels (pediococcus makes beer sour, but also produces nasty diacetyl; this strain had the sour without the smell), so he cultured it and today uses it in about half of his 200 or so projects. Short of capturing your own rogue bacteria, try these tips from Andy:

"**Think about the barrel as another ingredient.** You want it to complement the beer. If you're aging in wine barrels, keep the astringency of your beer low. Think dark and smooth, like a Baltic porter. You could take a blonde ale and chuck it in a wine barrel, but then you might as well just drink wine. With rum or bourbon, go with thick stouts."

"**If you buy new oak, it can take so long to get the oak flavor down.** The first batches will taste like chewing on oak. I'd put a beer in there, make another batch in a glass carboy, and then blend the 2 after 3 months. Blending is key."

"**If you're putting a saccharomyces-fermented beer in a barrel, your biggest enemy is oxygen.** Wood is porous, and oxidized beer tastes like cardboard, so less time in the barrel is better. With a fresh bourbon barrel, say, you can probably get all the flavor you need out of it in less than a month."

"**We take the Cantillon approach.** [The famous Belgian lambic brewery never dumps a batch.] Even if the beer tastes horrendous, we just let it sit. We have tons of barrels that 6 months in, my tasting notes all say, 'This tastes terrible—will probably dump.' But we never do, and it always turns a corner."

Sour Beers

THE BACKSTORY

Intensely debated, defined, and redefined, sours are some of the most misunderstood beers out there. Making a true, traditional lambic or a Flanders red or brown means following textbooks of rules (What kind of wheat? How old are the hops? How long is the boil?) and leaving the rest up to the mysteries of wild yeast, wood, and weather. Breweries superstitiously preserve their cobwebs; an Indian summer can ruin a beer years in the making.

Of course, in the old days (lambic recipes go back to the 1300s), sour beers were just beer—made in the only way that worked: brewed from the winter harvest and leftover hops, fermented naturally, then left to sit in old barrels until smooth enough to drink. All sour beers get their trademark tang from wild bacteria. The beers differ mainly in the technique with which they're made.

REDS, BROWNS, AND LAMBICS

Flanders reds and browns, acidic and vinegary, are made from malted barley, usually a medium-kilned variety like Vienna or Munich, and occasionally a little sugar. They're fermented with normal beer yeast at first, then aged with bacteria—especially acetobacter and lactobacillus—either in wood (reds) or stainless steel (browns, also called oud bruins). They're a bit sweet, and very sour.

Lambic is a seasonal beer. Brewers make a wort of pale malt and wheat in the winter and leave it out overnight to pick up a host of wild yeasts. They'll ferment it in a barrel with traditional beer yeast, but as spring and summer come and things warm up, the souring bacteria and wild yeast, like brettanomyces, that had been dormant in the wort take over. Lambics are hopped heavily, but only for preservative purposes, to keep the bacteria somewhat in check as the beer ages for years on end. Real lambic is flat and dry; if it's sweet, bubbly, or fruity, it's one of these:

- FARO is a lambic with sugar added.

- GUEUZE is a blend of old, dry lambics with young, sweet ones—the yeast from the old eats the sugars still left in the young and carbonates it.

- Adding cherries to a lambic as it ages makes a KRIEK; raspberries make FRAMBOISE, blackcurrants make a CASSIS.

WILD BACTERIA

Lambics, reds, and browns have some of the most complex fermentations in the world, with literally hundreds of different species of critters munching away on their sugars and producing sour acids that, over time, combine with alcohol and mellow into fruity esters that balance the beer's vinegary bite with notes of blackcurrant, banana, and grape. Yeah, it's complicated, but here's a lineup of the main players at work:

- ACETOBACTER: This bacteria makes acetic acid and gives sour beers their sharpest, vinegary edge.

- BRETTANOMYCES: This wild yeast's name means "British brewing industry fungus"—it was discovered in porters in 1904. There are many kinds, each with its own unique flavors, but the two most common are Bruxellensis, which is often described as horsey or barnyard-like, and Claussenii, which is drier and fruitier, like wine. These guys are slow, but thorough. In time, they'll chomp through almost every sugar in the beer, leaving the final product bone dry and super flavorful.

- LACTOBACILLUS: This bacteria makes lactic acid, which is a bit milder than acetic acid—more tangy than sharp.

- PEDIOCOCCUS: Another lactic acid producer, pediococcus is a bit more resilient than lactobacillus and can live even in highly hopped lambics.

MAKING YOUR OWN

For the past seven centuries, those bugs floated into breweries and barrels from neighboring orchards and fields. Today, you can buy ready-made vials of them, which means: Yes, you can make a sour beer at home. But it's not easy. Of course, the beauty of homebrewing is, you don't have to follow any rules—if it tastes good, you made it right.

BEERS TO TRY New Belgium Eric's Ale, Green Flash Super Freak, Russian River Supplication, Jolly Pumpkin Luciérnaga, Kuhnhenn Cherry Oud Bruin.

Tyler King, Head Brewer
THE BRUERY

Here's a simple process from Tyler King, head brewer at SoCal's The Bruery. He's been making sours professionally and at home ever since tasting his first Lindemans framboise. The first Flemish reds he brewed were nothing like the sweet cherry kriek, but he liked them even better: rich, flavorful, and loaded with wild funk. They're intense to drink, but making sours demands more patience than skill.

The key to making a good sour, Tyler says, is using good bacteria, then letting it shine. Grain bills on the original lambics and Flemish sours were simple, and yours should be, too:

- Measure 2 pounds of American 2-Row malt and either ½ pound of Vienna malt or Munich malt for a Flanders sour or ½ pound of wheat for a lambic.

- Mash at 153°F, then turn off the heat and let your mash sit overnight. This is called making a "sour mash," and you'll see why the next morning. The wild lactic bacteria naturally growing on the grains will have sprouted, and your mash will smell terrible. That's okay! Skim off any mold, drain it, and sparge with very hot water (180°F). Now boil as usual, hopping with about 14 grams of mild hops at the start.

- At this point, because of the sour mash, your beer will have a slight sour edge to it, but the boil will have killed any remaining lactic bacteria that would've developed those flavors further. To get some true bite, ferment with a normal yeast strain (called a neutral fermentation), rack into a secondary fermenter, and add a lactic culture. One without brettanomyces will keep your beer on the sweeter side.

- Some cultures, like Tyler's favorite, Wyeast Roeselare, contain regular brewing yeast in addition to wild bacteria. These should be pitched like normal ale yeast, and don't require you to pitch anything else once you rack to secondary. Add wood chips or fruit, if you like, and wait. After months, or even years, you'll have made one of the most revered and complicated beers in the world. Now drink it!

RON JEFFRIES

FOUNDER AND BREWMASTER, JOLLY PUMPKIN ARTISAN ALES

When you're brewing with unpredictable wild yeast, what can you do to make sure your beer turns out the way you want it to every time?

You brew good-tasting sour beers the same way you brew any other good tasting beer. It's not just thrown in a barrel and put in a bottle. It's about picking the right ingredients, practicing good sanitation. The wild yeast we have follows patterns. We just try to create an environment that the yeast is happy with, and set it on its path to make great beer.

What sorts of patterns?

We have one 2,000-liter barrel, and every November it'll produce ethyl acetate. I don't know if it's the nights getting colder, or the heater coming on in the brewery, or what, but we can't leave a beer in there for more than three weeks in November. We learned that the hard way. We had to dump 2,000 liters of beer. But if you're a professional brewer and you haven't dumped a batch, you've probably sold some substandard beer. Stuff always happens.

Do you have any superstitions, like saving cobwebs or anything?

We don't throw salt over our shoulders, but I have a lot of superstitions. When we rip open grain bags to pour the grain into our mash tun, we save all the tear-strings from the bags until the mash is over. We threw them away early one time, and we got a stuck mash. I leave the cobwebs up, but I'm not superstitious about it. The spiders help keep fruit flies out of the beer. Plus, we have a lot of high rafters, and they're just tedious to clean.

Do you feel like you have to educate people about sour beer?

The market for sour beers has a long way to go. I still get e-mails from people saying, I bought a bottle and had to dump it out because it had gone sour. But I look at it as an artist—that's very different from an evangelist. I brew the way I do for me, to create something beautiful and wonderful: the ever-elusive perfect beer. Every instant has its own perfect beer, and then it's gone. That's the fleeting art of the brewmaster.

DEXTER, MICHIGAN
EST. 2004
SIZE: 1,000 barrels/year
OUR FAVORITES: Bam Noir, Luciérnaga, La Roja, Oro de Calabaza

Jolly Pumpkin's sour beers are made in a low, white building outside of Ann Arbor, practically unmarked beyond the brewery logo stenciled in spray paint on a trash can out front. The building is filled with barrels. Rows and rows of them, some labeled in chalk with names like "C-Dog" and "Dos Loco" or just, cryptically, "Beast." Some barrels quietly bubble over with foam. Every once in a while, a stopper will blow out with a loud pop. It's a little creepy. Presiding over this alchemy is Ron Jeffries, appropriately nicknamed "Captain Spooky." He started Jolly Pumpkin in 2004 to make beers few Americans were making: sour ales, fermented in barrels with wild yeast. Part science, part art, it's a tradition as old as brewing gets, and Ron's beers capture that early magic, when fermentation was a mystery and every batch was different. History, it turns out, tastes incredible.

— Chapter Three —
DRINK

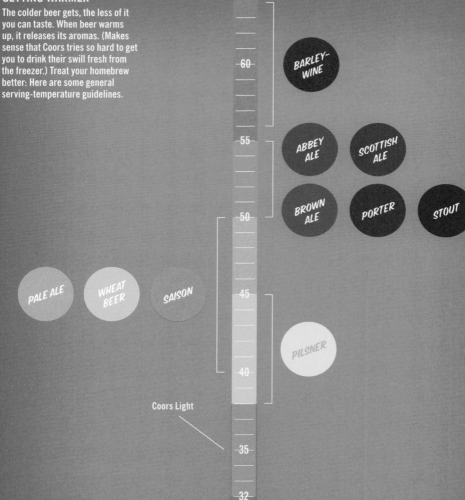

GETTING WARMER

The colder beer gets, the less of it you can taste. When beer warms up, it releases its aromas. (Makes sense that Coors tries so hard to get you to drink their swill fresh from the freezer.) Treat your homebrew better: Here are some general serving-temperature guidelines.

BARLEY-WINE

ABBEY ALE

SCOTTISH ALE

BROWN ALE

PORTER

STOUT

PALE ALE

WHEAT BEER

SAISON

PILSNER

Coors Light

60

55

50

45

40

35

32

°F

Beer can be as profound as fine wine, but that's rarely how people talk about it.

We think that's because your first sip of Bordeaux was probably cele-bratory, meant to savor, while your first beer was probably, let's just say, in high school. Savoring was not a priority. By now, though, you know something about how beer is made, and what makes it taste the way it does. But beyond that "why" of taste, you still need to learn the "how." Tasting beer might seem hard at first because beer can be so simple— just four ingredients—which leads some people to limit their vocabulary accordingly: malty, hoppy, light, strong. The truth is, those ingredients combine to create hundreds of different flavors, and the secret to tast-ing beer is being able to identify those flavors—even when your eyes may tell you they shouldn't be there. That pitch-black stout doesn't look like a bacon-and-coffee breakfast, but it just might taste like one.

THE PROPER POUR

SERVING TEMPERATURE Before you taste, you have to pour, but before you pour, check the temperature. If you've been raised on American beer ads, chances are, you're quaffing too cold. Pilsners and pale lagers should be a refreshing 38°F to 45°F, but darker beers like stouts and porters start to release their malty aromas closer to 50°F, and the strongest of the strong—barleywines, old ales, imperial stouts—can be even warmer. If you're out of fridge space or looking for long-term storage, it's best to keep your beers at what are called "cellar tempera-tures." Think basement, not closet: about 55°F.

What about the Yeast?

Many German bartenders will dribble that sediment over the frothy head of a weissbier as an accent. It's packed with B vitamins that some say help with hangovers, so don't worry about drinking it—it may even be good for you. Of course, if you're in hangover territory, you're probably not worried about a little yeast in your glass anyway.

PICK YOUR GLASS Lighter, bubblier beers like wheats and pilsners are best served in tall, thin glasses that show off their color and hold up a nice, thick head. For darker stuff, go short and wide—let it warm up and dissipate its foam. Check the chart on page 132, then it's time to pour.

POURING You probably think you know how to pour a beer perfectly, after seeing countless bartenders do it for you: Tilt the glass, pour down the side. It's fast, foam-free—and the exact opposite of what you should do. Beer's foam is unique, and so physically complicated that scientists are still studying it (taking beer into space, even, to look at foam in zero gravity). The proteins in beer create a kind of scaffolding that flavors, aromas, and foam ride on. When the scaffolding is really dense, it distributes carbon dioxide gas thinly and evenly, making for a creamier beer. We call that body, or mouth-feel. When poured right, even lightly carbonated English browns and pales (if they're made well) will support a fine head. Nitrogen doesn't dissolve as well as carbon dioxide in beer, instead creating tiny bubbles that make beers as thick and rich as milkshakes. You'll sometimes see heavier stouts served from specially outfitted nitrogen taps.

All of this is to say, foam matters. Pouring beer down the side of a glass hides a beer's carbonation, which hides its body and muddles its aroma. So be bold! Pour straight down the middle. (Warning: Any speck of dust, or soap, or grease, or grime can instantly kill even the best heads of foam. Hence the phrase "beer-clean glass," meaning totally and completely empty!) Now, on to the beer itself.

TASTING BEER

Start with the basics: What does it look like? How thick is the foam? What does it smell like? Think of the raw materials—grain bins at the homebrew store, packets of fresh hops—and try to match one of those memories to the beer. Now take a sip and think beyond the obvious ingredients. What foods come to mind? Biscuits and honey, maybe—or a shaker of black pepper. Flowers? It might seem cute, but the truth is, hops contain many of the same scent-producing oils as flowers (geraniol, from geraniums, is common in Cascades). Imagine a garden or a spice rack, and try to connect those scents to what you're drinking. Like anything, it takes practice—but, hey, you get to train at the bar! First, learn what can go wrong by identifying and fixing the occasional off flavors in your homebrew, then focus on the positive: picking out all the delicious flavors that combine to make your beer great.

BEERS GONE WRONG

We hate this part, but it must be said: Sometimes, things go wrong. You're homebrewing to make great beer, but also to make new and exciting beer, and that demands some risk. Remember: Every problem has a solution, but sometimes the solutions just have to wait until your next batch. Taste your beer as it's fermenting, so you can identify and solve these problems as they come up. If you're too late—the beer's in bottles and even the dog won't lap it up—don't dump it yet. Funny things have been known to happen to the sourest of batches if left alone for a while in the back of the fridge or in a cool, dark closet. Crack open another one in a month, and see if it's improved. No? Then all you can do is keep good notes, an open mind, and try again next time! What follows is a handy chart for identifying and rectifying problems in your homebrews.

MY BEER TASTES LIKE...	WHY? AND HOW DO I FIX IT?
APPLE PEELS GREEN-APPLE JOLLY RANCHERS UNRIPE PEACHES	**ACETALDEHYDE.** This is a natural by-product of fermentation, and yeast will eat it back up if given the chance. You might have bottled too early, separating the beer from the yeast too soon. **SOLUTION:** If there's any live yeast left in your bottles, it might take care of itself. Take the bottles out of the fridge, shake up the yeast, and let them sit for a week or two.
BAND-AIDS A MEDICINE CABINET	**CHLOROPHENOL.** A phenol, or aromatic compound, built with chlorine atoms. **SOLUTION:** If you're using chlorine-based sanitizers, stop! Or at least rinse your equipment better.

MY BEER TASTES LIKE...	WHY? AND HOW DO I FIX IT?
BUTTERSCOTCH BUTTERED POPCORN	**DIACETYL.** This is another chemical produced during fermentation, especially if you ferment too hot, which overworks the yeast. (There's an outside chance your beer is contaminated with pediococcus bacteria, but that'd cause other problems as well: smelly, sour gym socks.) **SOLUTION:** Wait a few more days before bottling. If you're brewing a lager, try a diacetyl rest (see page 43).
CANNED CORN TOMATO PLANTS COOKED CABBAGE OR VEGGIES	**DIMETHYL SULFIDE (DMS).** This is produced by so-called "wort-spoiler" bacteria. They love wort but hate beer—the low pH kills them. A good, fast fermentation is the best way to avoid these baddies. **SOLUTION:** Boil longer and stronger, and make sure to aerate your wort well after pitching your yeast.
CARDBOARD SHERRY (IN DARKER BEERS) ROTTEN PINEAPPLE GARBAGE	**OXIDATION.** Oxygen combined with alcohols produces staling compounds called aldehydes. **SOLUTION:** Keep air out! Fill your bottles and your fermenters as full as you can and try not to shake up or aerate hot wort.
CHEMICAL SOLVENTS NAIL-POLISH REMOVER OVERRIPE FRUIT	**ESTERS.** Sometimes you want to taste esters in small amounts—in a Belgian beer, say—but in most ales the flavor just overpowers your hops and malt. Belgian yeasts, and most other yeasts if they're overworked—by underpitching or fermenting too hot—will produce esters. **SOLUTION:** Pitch enough yeast, and make sure to aerate your wort well to help your yeast get to work quickly.
SOUR MILK VINEGAR	**ACETIC ACID** or **LACTIC ACID.** A little acid is okay in some beers, but probably not what you were hoping for. The bugs that sour beer do all sorts of other nasty things, so if your beer is hazy, thick, or buttery, as well as sour, you've been hit bad. **SOLUTION:** Sanitize better next time, and make sure to keep your fermenter tightly sealed against invaders.
SOY SAUCE RUBBER	**SULFUR.** When yeast dies, or autolyzes, it releases lots of nasty chemicals. **SOLUTION:** Rack or bottle your beer sooner, and try to minimize the amount of yeast you rack in your bottles.
SUGAR	**MALTOSE.** You're not done fermenting! Scotch ales and some stronger beers should be fairly sweet, but if your IPAs and porters are sugary, you're not letting them ferment long enough. **SOLUTION:** Keep an eye on your gravity, and let your beers ferment all the way down to the target final gravity.
A TEA BAG (ASTRINGENT; MAKES ME PUCKER)	**TANNINS.** Squeezing the mash in your grain bag or sparging with water that's too hot will pull out bitter tannins from your malt. **SOLUTION:** Be gentler with your mash—don't over-stir, and make sure your sparge water is under 170°F. You might want to check your tap water's pH, too—it may be high.

MY BEER...	WHY? AND HOW DO I FIX IT?
SMELLS LIKE CHEESE	**OXIDIZED HOPS.** Old hops smell like the opposite of fresh hops: stale and stinky when they should be fresh and sharp. **SOLUTION:** Store your hops as airtight as you can. If they smelled bad fresh from the store, take them back for a replacement (be nice).
SMELLS LIKE ROTTEN EGGS	**HYDROGEN SULFIDE.** Your beer might be infected, or just too young—especially if it's a lager. **SOLUTION:** Sanitize! If you're making a lager, wait a week or so to see if it dissipates.
SMELLS LIKE A SKUNK	**LIGHTSTRUCK.** When certain light waves hit certain hop molecules, they break them apart, and the pieces combine with hydrogen sulfide to produce the exact same compound skunks make. **SOLUTION:** Keep your beer away from light.
LOOKS LIKE A GEYSER	**INFECTION.** Foaming bottles are a classic sign that your beer has been infected with wild yeast. If you don't notice any characteristic wild sourness, you might just be over-priming your bottles. Or, there's a slim chance your malt may be moldy. **SOLUTION:** Sanitize! And/or use less priming sugar.
LOOKS HAZY	**SUSPENDED PROTEINS.** This is an obnoxious but merely aesthetic problem. Proteins that didn't settle out in your hot and cold breaks re-suspend when your beer is chilled. **SOLUTION:** Sometimes just letting the beer warm up will help, but permanent "chill haze" can only be beat by boiling your wort strongly and cooling it fast.
IS THIN	**NOT ENOUGH PROTEINS.** Other proteins (not the haze-making kind) are there to give your beer body. **SOLUTION:** Use more grains, especially an ounce or two of protein-rich wheat, and mash shorter and hotter to make a richer wort.
IS FLAT	**UNDER-CARBONATED.** When carbonating your beer naturally—that is, with active yeast, not a CO_2 pump—it can take some tweaking to get that perfect layer of foam. **SOLUTION:** Use a few more grams of bottling sugar, and try adding an ounce of flaked wheat to your mash.
IS THICK, SYRUPY, JELLY-LIKE, ROPY	**MAJOR INFECTION!** Acetobacter and pediococcus bacteria can produce a polysaccharide slime that disgusts even the bug-loving Belgians. Ropy beer was the most common complaint in Victorian England, when beers were subject to some of the nastiest air around. Thankfully, it's rarer today. **SOLUTION:** Sanitize!

Lauren Salazar
Sensory Trainer and Blender
NEW BELGIUM BREWING CO.

Gwen Conley
Quality Assurance/Sensory Director
FLYING DOG BREWERY

Now that you know what can go wrong, teach yourself how to recognize everything that goes right. Lauren Salazar started and runs the beer evaluation program at New Belgium Brewing (see page 134), where she trains everyone in the company to taste beer like a pro. Gwen Conley, who does the same thing at Flying Dog, came up with this tasting quiz, which Lauren uses to keep her brewers sharp.

The idea is to hard-wire flavor associations to help you pick out the individual notes that combine to make beer so complex. Those notes can be as obvious as the aroma of the beer's main base malt, or as subtle as the slight banana bloom of a hefeweizen. Smelling them one by one like this will build muscle memory, so when you order (or brew) that weissbier, say, you don't have to rack your brain to remember, oh, right: cloves! Here's how to play:

- Get a few little jars, put a couple drops or crumbs of the flavor or food specified in each one and pack in a cotton ball to absorb and contain the scent.

- Cover the jars, number them, and grab a pad and pencil.

- Open each jar, take a whiff, and scribble down your thoughts. Check your notes against these pages to see how you did.

We've included some information about what causes each flavor—some are delicious in beer, and some are signs of a problem—but the important thing is being able to identify them. Explaining them, and in the case of off flavors, fixing them, comes later. For now, have fun.

1 ALMOND EXTRACT

Benzaldehyde, a chemical precursor to alcohol, common in under-fermented or oxidized beers

2 BANANA FLAVOR

Isoamyl acetate, an ester considered good in some wheat beers but bad in most other ales

7 COCOA POWDER

Dark-roasted malts or real chocolate added to the beer

8 COFFEE GROUNDS

Dark-roasted malts or real coffee added to the beer

13 HONEY

Honey malts, beer with honey added (like braggot), or slightly oxidized beer

14 LIQUID SMOKE

Smoked malt or phenols produced by some yeasts

19 ROOT BEER

Some spiced beers, especially those with cardamom

20 ROSE GERANIUM OIL

Geraniol, an oil in Cascade, Sterling, Centennial, and other floral hops

25 CASCADE HOPS

The classic citrusy hop, popular in American pale ales

26 SAAZ HOPS

The classic spicy hop, popular in pilsners

3

BLACK PEPPER

Some beers have pepper added, others, like saisons, just use yeasts that produce peppery aromas

4

BUTTERED POPCORN

Diacetyl, the plague of lagers, caused by under-fermentation or bacterial contamination from pediococcus

5

CARDBOARD (WET)

Old, stale, or oxidized beer

6

CLOVES

A phenol, or aromatic compound, common in weissbier

9

DATES (OR RAISINS)

Some dark Crystal malts have these flavors already, but they get more pronounced as the beer ages

10

DISH SOAP

Smoked malt, or phenols produced by some yeasts

11

DRIED MUSHROOMS

Very, very old, musty beer, usually caused by barrel-aging

12

GRAHAM CRACKERS

Biscuity aromas from some malts

15

NAIL-POLISH REMOVER

Ethyl acetate, a strong ester almost always problematic, except in tiny amounts

16

ORANGE EXTRACT

Fruit or sweet orange peel added, as in some wheat beers

17

PARMESAN CHEESE

Old, stale hops

18

PINE

Myrcene, a piney oil in hops like Chinook

21

VANILLA EXTRACT

Common in beers aged in oak

22

VEGEMITE (OR TAMARI)

Dead, autolyzed yeast

23

VINEGAR

Acetobacter, a bacteria common in Flemish sour beers

24

WHISKEY

Alcoholic warmth from strong or bourbon-barrel-aged beers

27

PALE ALE MALT

A common base malt in ales

28

PILSNER MALT

A common base malt in lagers and Belgian ales

29

40°L CRYSTAL MALT

Lightly sweet and bready malt common in amber ales and brown ales

30

120°L CRYSTAL MALT

Rich, sweet malt common in dark beers like Scottish ales and doppelbocks

Amy Van Arsdale
Cheesemonger
BEDFORD CHEESE SHOP

Who dares split up wine and cheese? That stodgy pair has lorded over hors d'oeuvres tables for eons (and the cheese usually looks like it). It's supposed to be high-class, but let's face it: Unless you *really* know what you're doing, the cheese is too sweet or too rich, the wine too tannic or too thin. The cheese, in other words, is always too cheesy, and the wine . . . you get the idea. But beer is forgiving! Light or thick, sharp or smooth, it always seems to balance whatever you throw at it. It figures—beer is basically bread, and what makes more sense than cheese on toast?

Amy Van Arsdale, cheesemonger at Bedford Cheese Shop in Brooklyn paired each of our basic beers with some of her favorite American cheeses. For bigger appetites, she's also suggested a few whole meals to build around your beer.

CHEESES TO TRY

YOUR BEER

FOODS TO PAIR

Cheese Plate

TRY SOMETHING
FRUITY, YEASTY & BRINY

- Point Reyes Farmstead Original Blue
- Rogue Creamery Rogue River Blue
- 5-Spoke Creamery Tumbleweed

Dinner Menu

TRY SOMETHING
LIGHT, SIMPLE & SUMMERY

- Roast chicken with lots of herbs
- Vegetable couscous
- Gazpacho

PALE ALE

Cheese Plate

TRY SOMETHING
NUTTY & SLIGHTLY SWEET

- Major Farm Vermont Shepherd
- 3-Corner Field Farm Battenkill Brebis
- Thistle Hill Farm/Spring Brook
  Farm Tarentaise

Dinner Menu

BROWN ALE

TRY SOMETHING
DARK & FLAVORFUL
BUT NOT TOO HEAVY

- Meatloaf
- Burgers
- Simple vegetable stew

Cheese Plate

TRY SOMETHING
TOASTED, CARAMELY & SMOKY

- 3-Corner Field Farm Frère Fumant
- Uplands Pleasant Ridge Reserve
- Holland's Family Farm Marieke Gouda
- Cypress Grove Midnight Moon

Dinner Menu

PORTER

TRY SOMETHING
RICH WITH A SWEET EDGE

- Thick-cut pork chops with apples
- Steak with caramelized onion jam

Cheese Plate

TRY SOMETHING
CREAMY, SHARP & EARTHY

- Bleu Mont Dairy Bandaged Cheddar
- Cabot Creamery Clothbound Cheddar
- Sprout Creek Farm Ouray

Dinner Menu

STOUT

TRY SOMETHING
RICH, THICK & HEARTY

- Beef stew
- Chili with dark Baltic rye bread

SCOTTISH ALE

Cheese Plate

TRY SOMETHING
EARTHY, BLOOMY & MUSHROOMY

- Twig Farm Square Cheese
- Consider Bardwell Farm Chester
- Cowgirl Creamery Mt. Tam

Dinner Menu

TRY SOMETHING
CREAMY & EARTHY

- Shepherd's pie
- Lamb, duck, or venison sausage

WHEAT BEER

Cheese Plate

TRY SOMETHING
BRIGHT, TANGY & FRESH

- Local mozzarella, burrata, or fresh chèvre
- 3-Corner Field Farm Brebis Blanche
- Redwood Hill Farm Goat Feta

Dinner Menu

TRY SOMETHING
YOUNG, FRESH & GREEN

- Spring salad with heirloom tomatoes, pole beans, cucumber, and corn
- Pasta with spring vegetables

SAISON

Cheese Plate

TRY SOMETHING
FLUFFY, TANGY & LIGHT

- Cherry Glen Farm Monocacy Ash
- Capriole Farm Sofia
- Lazy Lady Farm Valençay

Dinner Menu

TRY SOMETHING
LIGHT, FRIED & CITRUSY

- Fried fish with lemon
- Pork schnitzel

Cheese Plate

TRY SOMETHING
PUNGENT, MEATY & FRUITY

- Haystack Mountain Farm Sunlight
- Meadow Creek Farm Grayson
- Consider Bardwell Farm Manchester

Dinner Menu

TRY SOMETHING
CREAMY & SMOKY

- Risotto with bacon, peas, and leeks

ABBEY ALE

Cheese Plate

TRY SOMETHING
SOFT & DELICATE

- 3-Corner Field Farm Shushan Snow
- Redwood Hill Farm Camelia
- Nettle Meadow Farm Kunik

Dinner Menu

TRY SOMETHING
SPICY & RICH

- Pretzels with spicy German mustard
- Harissa olives
- Chorizo tacos
- Thai curry

PILSNER

Cheese Plate

TRY SOMETHING
SALTY, SAVORY & NUTTY

- Wisconsin Sheep Dairy Cooperative Dante
- Roelli Cheese Haus Dunbarton Blue
- Rogue River Creamery Echo Mountain

Dessert Menu

TRY SOMETHING
SWEET & RICH

- Ginger or molasses cookies with pumpkin or chocolate ice cream (make your own ice cream sandwich)
- Spiced pear or apple tart

BARLEY-WINE

SHAKER PINT

TULIP PINT

NONIC PINT

SNIFTER

TULIP

GOBLET

SHAKER PINT Originally used to shake cocktails, but filled with beer starting in the 1980s. Never ideal, but okay for most ales—straight sides and a large mouth means the beer gets warm and flat fast, which can show off the malty notes of some English-style ales.

SNIFTER The small mouth concentrates aroma (a snobbish swirl or two helps even more) but minimizes foam. Pour barleywines, quads, eisbocks, and big stouts, and let the beer warm up a bit in your hand.

TULIP PINT The classic for Guinness and other dry stouts. According to Guinness, a perfect, two-part pour that lets the head rest before topping off should take exactly 119.53 seconds.

TULIP A cinched mouth focuses aromatics but opens up at the lip to support a foamy head. Great for saisons, Scotch ales, Belgian strongs, and big IPAs—anything flavorful that you don't dare drink a lot of.

NONIC PINT That bump keeps it from chipping (hence, "no-nick"). They're often marked with a fill line these days, to encourage pouring with a 1-inch head. This wasn't always the case, and bartenders would fill them right to the rim, or face the consequences. Fine for most ales.

GOBLET Keeping your grip low on the stem helps the beer stay cold. A wide mouth dissipates carbonation fast, letting strong abbey beers show off their flavor.

PILSNER GLASS

WEIZEN VASE

FLUTE

STEIN

SEIDEL

LITTLE GLASSES

PILSNER GLASS Narrow, to show off the pale-as-straw color; tapered, to hold up thick foam.

STEIN Big and heavy for holding a lot of beer and keeping it cold. The lid protects it from bugs while boozing in outdoor beer gardens. Pour the classics: pilsners, märzens, helles bocks, and Oktoberfests.

WEIZEN VASE Like a pilsner glass, tall and tapered to maximize head. A traditional weizen pour involves inverting the bottle completely over the glass and letting the beer glug out in one quick, foam-enhancing stream.

SEIDEL Like a lidless glass stein, but with etched (now usually molded) dimples to play with light shining through pale beers.

FLUTE Just like with champagne, the shape preserves bubbles. Good for effervescent gueuzes and saisons.

LITTLE GLASSES Schnitt glasses held chasers, offered automatically in early-1900s America. Pokal glasses, great for strong bocks, are tapered to show off a nice head. Stange (also called rod) glasses are meant to keep Kölschs very cold. Dwarf glasses—meant for super-strong October beers or barleywines—were popular among 18th- and 19th-century English aristocrats.

LAUREN SALAZAR

SENSORY TRAINER AND BLENDER, NEW BELGIUM BREWING CO.

You started working at New Belgium in 1997 as an office assistant—never in the brewery. How'd you go from that to running the tasting operation?
I'm not a brewer. I've never brewed a thing in my life. But I'm really good at asking brewers to make things for me—I tell them what it should taste like, what it should smell like, the mouthfeel, and the brewmaster translates it into things like kilograms of Munich malts. And I noticed that every day when we'd do a taste panel, there'd just be a pitcher of beer in an ice bucket, scraps of paper and pens. I was like, This beer has been sitting here for hours! They said, Well, if you can do it better, then do it. So I said, Okay, I will.

But brewing is such a science—why was the tasting so ad hoc?
In the food science world, you can go into a place like a cracker factory and this is what it looks like. A lab. But with brewing, strangely, as we advanced technologically, we replaced tasting with IBUs and spectrographs and—oh, crud—we forgot to taste the beer.

Are you born with a good palate, or can you learn it?
It's all training. But the problem with flavor training is you're starting at zero. So to go from that to saying this molecule is making that flavor—no one ever taught you that. It's scary! As kids, we start out with a box of eight Crayolas: This is red, this is blue. Then you got to 16, and you're saying, This is magenta, this is periwinkle. But no one did that for you with your tomato soup and grilled cheese.

Does being a flavor expert ruin regular old drinking?
When I was just starting to get into beers, I loved Red Hook ESB because it was sweet and yummy, like butterscotch. Now I know that was because it had diacetyl in it. They've since fixed it, but when you know a beer is teeming with bacteria, it tastes like an infection, and you can't unlearn that. Knowing how to taste beer definitely makes your beer budget go up. But the more people know, the better beer has to get.

FORT COLLINS, COLORADO
EST. 1991

SIZE: 650,000 barrels/year

OUR FAVORITES: Fat Tire, Abbey, Eric's Ale, Mothership Wit

Every day at New Belgium, 20 or so brewers, office assistants, bottling-line operators, and other employees file into Lauren Salazar's ground-floor lab to taste beer. It's a simple idea—make everyone with a stake in the beer responsible for making sure it tastes perfect, all the time—but was surprisingly uncommon when New Belgium started in 1991. Today, Lauren's sensory training program is one of the most extensive in the beer world. By crunching the numbers of those 20 daily tests, Lauren can track the flavor profiles of all New Belgium beers and tell if anything changes, or needs to change. Lucky for us, it rarely does. Beers like Abbey and Fat Tire, first brewed by founders Jeff Lebesch and Kim Jordan from scribbled notebook recipes and yeast smuggled back from a 1989 trip to Belgium, taste as great from one of the biggest craft breweries as they must have tasted when they were just batches of perfect homebrew.

Chapter Four

DESIGN

THINK OUTSIDE THE OVAL

The first beer labels were circles and ovals, then came rectangles, and there, for some reason, evolution stopped. You're your own bottling line, so use whatever shape you want, and change when you feel like it. Any of these silhouettes can make a label template if you scan and enlarge it by 300 percent.

Every great beer deserves a great bottle. Now that you've brewed yours, it's time to brand it. We think that's half the fun.

For almost as long as there have been breweries, there have been brewery imitators, and so beer was one of the first products on earth to be officially branded. German brewers started knocking off the Paulaner monastery's Salvator dark lager as soon as it was released in 1780, and continue to do so today, even after the Salvator name was trademarked in 1894—just count how many beers ending in "-ator" you see in the liquor store.

Under similar pressure, Bass's red triangle was trademarked in 1876, and Guinness's harp, Anheuser-Busch's eagle, and Ballantine's three rings soon followed.

Branding makes beer one-of-a-kind, but it can also make it part of a scene. Hand-drawn hop trellises and jokey puns? Gotta be an American craft brew. What yours will say is up to you. Take some inspiration from the pros—just promise not to copy!

BRAND YOUR BREWERY

BREWERY NAMING The first step towards branding can be as easy as using your own name or as, well, easy as looking out your window. Some breweries go biographic, others go geographic, but most don't look very much further for a name. The bar isn't necessarily low—nothing wrong with hometown pride—but there's plenty of room for bigger thinking.

▶ Name Game

Writer's block? Check the chart for a taxonomy of our favorite brewery names, and find inspiration for your own. Build on one of the categories here, or come up with a new one. The less obvious, the better, as far as we're concerned—half these breweries go with geography, and almost a quarter just use their birth certificate.

Be bold, but beware: Naming has a few potential pitfalls. "New" can fly (see: Albion, Belgium, and Glarus), but "Old" is out. In 1938, 115 brews were labeled as "old" versions of something else, including our favorite, Ohio's Old Gross.

BEER NAMING The effort saved on naming breweries gets spent on naming beers. We've come a long way from the days of San Francisco Brewing's Foamy Lager and plain white cans that just said "Beer." Take a cue from the pros: There are lots of puns ("hop" is such a useful syllable), lots of inside jokes (Tröegs's Flying Mouflan, anyone?), and lots of badass posturing (bastards, ruffians, dead guys). Of course, you could just call your beer what it is, but where's the fun in that?

LOGO DESIGN Many classic logos use the same handful of tropes: ribbons and scrolls, bunches of harvested hops and barley, and the ever-present eagle. Newer logos can tend towards the nautical, with anchors and sails alluding to beer's seafaring history. But in truth, that flash goes back to the earliest days of IPAs. The brewer's star, a mystical hexagram thousands of years old, has sadly fallen out of fashion. (Brooklyn's Sixpoint is an exception—they combine it with a nautical star to add a touch of local history.)

LABEL DESIGN Label designs are as just as varied as the beers they promote—from Stone's menacing gargoyles to Great Divide's slick silhouettes. Some are peppered with secret codes, like Rolling Rock's mysterious "33." Others change from batch to batch: Anchor has hired the same artist to illustrate a new Christmas Ale label every year since 1975.

Still, you'll see a few themes. Labels for dark lagers—called bocks—almost always feature a goat, a play on the town where they were first brewed, Einbeck, and the German for goat, *ein Bock*. Brown ales go well with dogs. Avery and Smuttynose both use a lazy chocolate Lab, but nothing's as cute as the old Los Angeles Brewing Company's "Simply Harmless Temperance Brew"—a measly 2 percent ABV near beer from the '30s, branded with a muzzled puppy.

Remember, a label is more than just space for a name. Some are

KNOW YOUR BREWERY TAXONOMY

ANIMALS	NATURE	GRAPHICS	ICONS	TYPE
DOG	SUN	STAR	CROWN	SANS SERIF
SQUIRREL	MOUNTAIN	BANNER	ANCHOR	SLAB SERIF
EAGLE	RIVER	SHIELD	KEY	SWASH
BEAR	HOPS	STRIPES	HORSESHOE	SHADOW
GOAT	BARLEY	SCROLL	TROPHY	OUTLINE

soapboxes for brewers' rants. Some, just space to gloat: Pabst's blue ribbon was first printed on their bottles in 1895—13 years, and more than a million yards of blue silk, after Pabst began tying them around bottle necks by hand.

In their heyday, when labels were as interesting as beer was bland, some were even interactive. Two Cleveland breweries used their packages to distract drinkers from what was inside them: One label had trivia on perforated strips, the other had a question printed on the outside and the answer on the inside, visible through the empty bottle.

Paper shortages in World War II Britain caused some brewers to print their labels directly onto glass, and a few craft brewers follow suit today—stymieing fidgety fingers and homebrewers hoping to strip and reuse the bottles.

Making these labels is simple, but designing them takes a bit of thought. So before you fire up your printer, think about what makes your homebrew unique, and what will help it stand out in your friends' refrigerators. Maybe that means beating the pros at their own game—geographic brewery name, jokey beer name, and a couple graceful hop vines twirling around an India-bound clipper. Or maybe it's just a quick scrawl with a Sharpie. Maybe every group of bottles will look as different as the batch of beer inside it, or maybe you dream of an empire: one logo binding bottles, t-shirts, coasters, the works. It's your beer—make sure everyone knows it.

◀ Branding Bingo

For more help with your brewery logo, mix and match imagery and typography styles from this handy chart. Some are common—Anheuser-Busch may have made the eagle and crown ubiquitous, but that's all the more reason to claim them as your own—and some just need a little love. (Bonus points if you use the squirrel!)

LABELS

MATERIALS

Bottles*
8½" x 11" printable
  sticker or label paper
Printer
Graphic design software
Scissors or X-acto knife

OPTIONS

Waterproof paper, or other
  specialty label material
Xyron 900 sticker machine
  with adhesive cartridge

SEE ALSO

beercraftbook.com
  for more ideas

*See page 31 for the best
way to remove label
adhesive from commercial
bottles.

Second only to a paint-pen tag, paper labels are the easiest way to brand your homebrew. Standard, rectangular labels are 3 inches high by 4 inches wide, and a pack of 15 sheets of letter-sized sticker paper will make about 90 labels. Step it up by playing with different shapes (see page 138 for templates) or adding a neck label (see right). Just scan in the template, enlarge it, color it in, and hit print.

Keep in mind that if you're brewing for a special occasion like a picnic or tailgate where your beer will be stashed in a cooler of ice, regular paper labels will run and fade when they get wet. You don't need waterproof ink—just waterproof paper. You can find that at most camping supply stores, where it's sold for printing all-weather maps.

If you use waterproof paper, or any other special stock—metallics, foils, photographs, fabrics—you'll have to apply your own glue. A high-strength glue stick works fine, but we like using a Xyron sticker machine. It's pricey (about $100), but a craft store staple. Wind the crank, and the machine will apply a thin layer of permanent adhesive to anything you feed through it. It's far from necessary, but consider it for your next bottling-line upgrade.

HEAD AND SHOULDERS

We love neck labels. They're unexpected flourishes and they come in way more shapes and styles than their more prominently located cousins down below. For a special twist, look to Orval, one of our favorite Trappist ales, and label your beer with nothing but. Try these templates, scanned and enlarged by 200 percent.

Cap

Collar

Neck

Shoulder

Body

Name Tag

Branding your beer can be as quick and painless as uncapping a silver Sharpie. Metallic permanent markers and oil-based-paint pens are great to have around your home brewery to keep your bottles in order. It only takes a few seconds to scribble down a name, style, and date. It's a good idea, especially if you plan on sharing. A pro brewer friend of ours still wonders who gave him the best homebrew he's ever tasted—the bottle came unmarked.

Gilt Edge Premium Beer

CONTENTS 12 FL. OZS. • BREWED & BOTTLED BY BOSCH BREWING CO., HOUGHTON, MICH.

Schoenling DRAFT BEER

KEG FRESH   KEEP COLD

BREWED AND BOTTLED BY THE SCHOENLING BREWING CO., CINTI., OHIO

NOT PASTEURIZED • NOT RESPONSIBLE FOR SPOILAGE

INTERNAL REVENUE TAX PAID   NET CONTENTS 11 FL. OZ.

FRONTIER BRAND BEER

KERN BREWING CO. • BAKERSFIELD, CALIFORNIA

MAIER BREWING COMPANY, LOS ANGELES, CALIF.   NET CONTENTS ONE FULL QUART

King Cole Premium Pale BEER

BOTTLED EXCLUSIVELY FOR KING COLE MARKETS

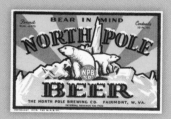

MAIER BREWING CO.—LOS ANGELES, CALIF.   NET CONTENTS 12 FLUID OUNCES BEER

Poli Dry BREW 102 Draught Beer Flavor

PERFECTED AFTER 101 BREWS

BREWED IN THE HEART OF THE FINGER LAKES

INTERNAL REVENUE TAX PAID   CONTENTS 12 FL. OZ.

Glen Ale

BREWED AND BOTTLED BY GLEN BREWING CO., INC.   WATKINS GLEN, NEW YORK

Pfeiffer PREMIUM ALE

Brewed & Bottled by Pfeiffer Brewing Company, Detroit, Mich.

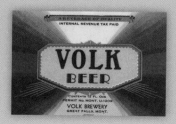

BEAR IN MIND   Contents 12 FL. OZ.

NORTH POLE BEER

NPB

THE NORTH POLE BREWING CO. FAIRMONT, W. VA.

INTERNAL REVENUE TAX PAID

CONTENTS ONE QUART

Katz Premium BEER

DREWRYS LTD. U.S.A. INC., SOUTH BEND, IND.

CONTENTS ONE FULL QUART   CONTENTS ONE FULL QUART

BAVARIAN flavor PILSNER BEER

MAIER BREWING CO. • LOS ANGELES, CALIF.

A BEVERAGE OF QUALITY   INTERNAL REVENUE TAX PAID

VOLK BEER

CONTENTS 12 FL. OZS.   PERMIT No. MONT. U-1209

VOLK BREWERY   GREAT FALLS, MONT.

NET CONTENTS ONE QUART

GOLDEN GATE Genuine DRAFT BEER

Maier Brewing Co., Los Angeles, Calif.

MAKE YOUR OWN

FIRED-ONS

MATERIALS

Bottles*
Sticker paper
Permanent marker
X-acto knife
Rubbing alcohol
Enamel paint, various
  colors (like DecoArt Gloss
  Enamels)
Foam paint brush, 2" wide
China markers

EQUIPMENT

Oven

SEE ALSO

beercraftbook.com
  for more ideas

*See page 31 for the best
  way to remove label
  adhesive from commercial
  bottles.

The original hope with "fired-on" or screen-printed bottles was that they'd be returned to the brewery for reuse. Check your recycling bin—obviously, that doesn't always happen. Still, they look cool, and since you'll be keeping better track of your homebrew (and reusing the bottles), it makes some sense to brand them this way. Just make sure to incorporate some white space into your design so you can write in batch names and brew dates.

First, decide on your design. Simpler is better, since you'll be stenciling them on. Think crisp, graphic shapes, like a simple logo or initial that symbolizes

your brewery. (If you have the time, you can hand-paint a design on each bottle individually.) One-color designs are easiest, since each color you add will require making another stencil (and more drying time).

Next, create your stencil. Draw or print your design onto sticker paper, and cut out the areas you want to print with an X-acto knife. You'll need as many stencils as bottles, since you'll leave them on while the paint dries. Doubly clean your bottles by wiping them down with rubbing alcohol, and stick on your stencils.

Using enamel paint and a foam brush, paint over each stencil in one, clean stroke. Let the paint dry, and add a second coat if you need to, before you remove the stencil. If you're using another color, take off the first stencil and apply the second, aligning the design as well as you can.

Once your design is complete and the paint has dried for 48 hours, bake the finished bottles in your oven to seal on the design. (That's why they're called fired-ons.) If you don't heat the glass, the paint may start to peel the next time you clean and sanitize your bottles—so it's worth the extra step.

Glass can shatter when it's heated or cooled too rapidly, so handle your bottles carefully. Put them in a cold oven, then set the temperature to 325°F so they'll heat up gradually. Bake them for 30 minutes—long enough to set the paint—then turn the oven off. Let them cool down to room temperature before you take them out.

When using your custom bottles to package your homebrew, be sure to note your beer's name (or style) and the brew date somewhere on the bottle.

China markers (which are like waxy colored pencils) are a great tool for this. You can write the batch-specific info directly on your painted label, then wash it off before you bottle your next batch. Or you can add batch-specific details to your caps (see page 150).

DESIGN YOUR OWN

BOTTLE CAPS

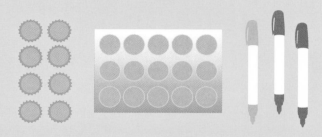

MATERIALS

Bottle caps, various colors
Metallic Sharpie markers
Oil-based-paint pens,
  various colors
Circular mailing stickers,
  1" diameter (like Avery
  #5249)

OPTIONS

Printer
Graphic design software

SEE ALSO

beercraftbook.com
  for more ideas

You need to buy new caps for each batch of beer you brew, so why not make them unique? Colored caps are a simple way to code your beer—yellow for pale ale, blue for stout, whatever. (The Trappist brewery Westvleteren uses only caps to distinguish between their beers—no labels at all.) Just be sure to record your packaging choices in your brew log. After a few weeks of carbonating and conditioning, it's easy to forget which batch is which.

If you want to get more creative, start with hand-drawn artwork. Metallic Sharpie markers and oil-based-paint pens are waterproof, so you can create your caps while your beer's still fermenting, then drop them in sanitizer solution on bottling day.

Stickers help you scale up your production. Look for printable mailing seals at any office supply store. One-inch circular labels are just about the right size, and metallic silver ones will blend into silver bottle caps perfectly. (Neither one is waterproof, so stick them on after the caps have been sanitized and crimped on your homebrew.) If you're going digital and printing your cap designs on stickers, it's easy to include lots of fun details. Think multi-colored logos, brew dates, or other Easter eggs. Use the next three pages as inspiration.

BEER CRAFT
BREWING CO.
Summer Lager
BOTTLED
6/26/10

PALE
ALE

Prosit!

100%
AMERICAN
2-ROW MALT
CASCADE HOPS
WLP001 YEAST

*MOMENTS IN
BEER HISTORY*
WILLIAM PAINTER
PATENTS
CROWN CAP
1892

SHANE C. WELCH

FOUNDER AND BREWMASTER, SIXPOINT CRAFT ALES

How do you come up with a recipe?

We've done extreme beers, but we don't go into a recipe with the desire to see how potent we can make something. We don't think of reinventing a classical style; we create a flavor profile and work from there. We reverse-engineer everything. We made one beer that we wanted to taste like an Alsatian wine, with a mineral pop, a grassy finish. For another one, we got 38 different strains of Japanese plums from a farm upstate. We tasted them, and we made a kind of plum wine, but as beer. It's so awesome.

Tell us about the steinbier you made—boiling the wort with red-hot rocks—something that brewers haven't done much of for hundreds of years.

We feel a fraternity with this really old craft of brewing, and we wanted to rouse that ancestral spirit. We brew with modern technology that we take for granted, and we wanted to troubleshoot this from a mechanical perspective, to learn about the rocks, the science behind it. We do that all the time. We have an archive of experiments we want to try.

So do you brew as a scientist?

Science and brewing go together so well—brewing is ripe for you to apply what you know about the physical world on a scale that really has an impact. But there's an art to science—a style to what you do. We still think with a lot of creativity and finesse. We try to brew efficiently, getting the flavors we want by changing our techniques. We build a lot of equipment. We're mad scientists.

Is there room for surprise in scientific brewing?

Four or five years ago, I was brewing, and I was a little behind, stressed. I pitched the wrong yeast by accident: a Belgian abbey yeast in our Bengali Tiger IPA. I realized it later that night when I was home, and I ran back. But it had already started fermenting. It turned out amazing, and we actually just brewed it again. That happens all the time—you'll make a mistake, and the final product will be better than what you imagined. So make sure to take notes!

BROOKLYN, NEW YORK

EST. 2004

SIZE: 13,000 barrels/year

OUR FAVORITES: Righteous Rye, (Double) Sweet Action, Diesel Stout, Gorilla Warfare Coffee Porter

Sixpoint doesn't make typical craft beers, if there is such a thing. There are no overloaded hop bombs here, nothing too sour or too strong. The beer is soft-spoken, but after the fourth (or fifth . . .) pint, something special: drinkable, and that's not a dirty word. Brewed in an old brick building on the water's edge of Brooklyn, Sixpoint beers are perfectly balanced, from the subtle Sweet Action cream ale to the richly satisfying Gorilla Warfare coffee porter. Shane Welch, a homebrewing Midwesterner with a chemistry degree and a tinkerer's restless spirit, started the brewery in 2004. He raises rare chickens on the roof, plays piano in his office, and builds his own brewing equipment downstairs. Which is to say, as composed as his beers are, they're far from simple.

Chapter Five

REPEAT

OUTFIT YOUR BREWERY AND LOG YOUR BREWS

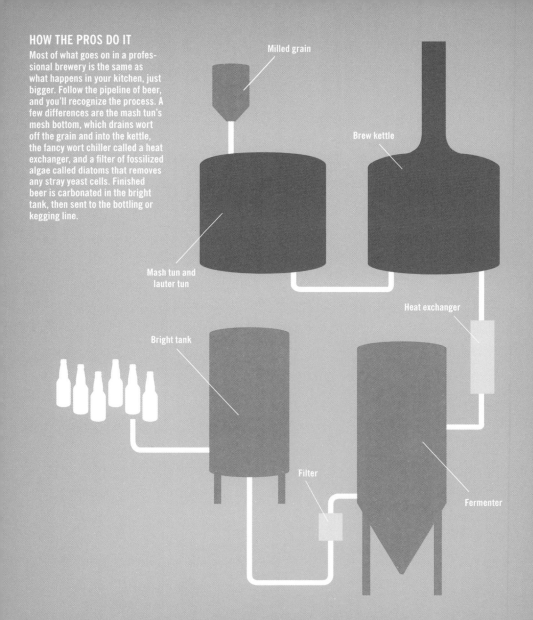

HOW THE PROS DO IT

Most of what goes on in a professional brewery is the same as what happens in your kitchen, just bigger. Follow the pipeline of beer, and you'll recognize the process. A few differences are the mash tun's mesh bottom, which drains wort off the grain and into the kettle, the fancy wort chiller called a heat exchanger, and a filter of fossilized algae called diatoms that removes any stray yeast cells. Finished beer is carbonated in the bright tank, then sent to the bottling or kegging line.

Milled grain

Brew kettle

Mash tun and lauter tun

Heat exchanger

Bright tank

Filter

Fermenter

You're hooked, right? Before you jump into batches 2 through 200, though, turn your kitchen into a proper home brewery by mastering your equipment, recording your brews, and stocking your library as well as your fridge.

You don't need the latest German steel fermenters or temperature-controlled brew kettles to make great beer—in fact, even a few of our favorite pro brewers improvise their gear from eBay finds and scrap metal—but there are bound to be a few items you'll have to buy. We've narrowed them down to the essentials, including tips on what to look for at the hardware store and some timesaving upgrades if you want to spend a little extra.

The most important piece of homebrewing equipment is a notebook. When we brew, we sometimes make things up as we go—substituting this hop for that one, adding a little smoked malt, throwing in a chili pepper. Recipes are just a place to start. But that doesn't mean you shouldn't take notes. Some of our best beers were accidents, but it always helps to know what we did right (or not so right). Keep a copy of these pages nearby as you brew, and write down everything. Had an unusually quick fermentation? Forgot to add bittering hops? You never know what will make this beer the one you'll want to brew again and again.

Finally, check the resources section for the best places to stock up on ingredients or just geek out over books of recipes and more advanced techniques. There's always more to learn about brewing, but more importantly, there's always more beer to brew.

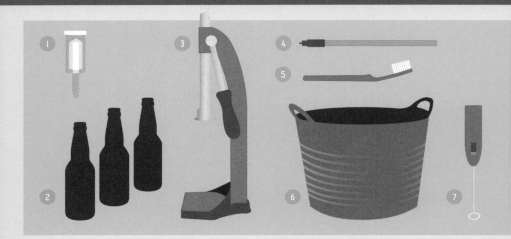

① AIRLOCK

There are two kinds of airlocks: an S-shaped bubbler and a three-piece. The bubbler is simpler to use—just fill with water and stick in the stopper—and it makes it easy to check whether your beer is producing CO_2 by glancing at the water-line. The three-piece, though, is much easier to clean if fermentation gets foamy.

② BOTTLES

These come in more shapes and sizes than you probably imagine (see BOTTLES BY SHAPE, inside front cover), but any is fine, as long as it's brown and not a twist-off. Swing-top Grolsch bottles are handy if you don't have a capper.

③ BOTTLE CAPPER

There are two types. The two-handed, winged version is more common, but we like the single-arm, bench-mounted style. It's easier to use, it looks cool on your kitchen counter, and you can usually find them for cheap at flea markets. Just be aware that some old cappers are too tall to cap stubby bottles.

④ BOTTLING WAND

Also known as a bottle filler, this device takes the place of a hose clamp when you bottle your beer. Attach it to one end of your siphon tubing. When the end of the wand hits the bottom of a bottle, it opens a valve and lets beer flow through. Helpful, but not necessary.

⑤ BRUSHES

Pipe cleaners, Q-Tips, and narrow, nylon brushes are great to have around to clean crud from fermenter necks, airlocks, and tubes.

⑥ BUCKET

Anything big enough to fit a few gallons of sanitizer and all your equipment.

⑦ CAPPUCCINO FOAMER

Not essential, but handy for quickly aerating your wort.

8 FERMENTERS & CARBOYS

We like one-gallon glass jugs because they let us see what our beer is doing. Buy some apple cider at the farmers market, a gallon of cheap wine, or check your local homebrew store. If you opt for a plastic bucket, make sure it's food-grade and has a tight-fitting lid. Drill a one-inch hole in the top for your stopper and airlock.

9 GRAIN BAG

A very fine mesh bag for holding all your grain during your mash. Make sure it's large enough—at least two gallons, or about 20 inches by 20 inches. Some homebrew shops will sell muslin grain bags, but opt for nylon if you can find it. The weave is finer (meaning fewer grain particles in your wort), and nylon bags last longer.

10 HOSE CLAMP

Indispensable for opening and closing your tubing while you bottle. Make sure it fits your bottling hose (½ inch outside diameter), and can click completely shut.

11 HYDROMETER & TUBE

Some hydrometers measure temperature as well, which is helpful considering a hydrometer reading is only accurate at 60°F. Whichever you choose, just be careful—these things break easily.

12 MEASURING CUP

You're going to be measuring water in pints and quarts, so larger measuring cups are best—make sure yours holds at least one pint.

13 RACKING CANE

A racking cane is essential for siphoning beer into bottles. They usually come long—built to fit five-gallon fermenters—and can be a little unwieldy in your one-gallon jug, so look for the shortest one you can find. Metal or plastic doesn't matter, but built-up gunk is easier to see and clean in clear ones. Take a step up with an auto siphon: a racking cane with a built-in suction chamber that starts a siphon without giving you a mouthful of sanitizer.

I BREW THE
BEER I DRINK

① REFRIGERATOR WITH TEMPERATURE CONTROLLER

Yes, we know, we promised gadget-free brewing. Skip this item if you want—we won't mind, and your beer won't suffer for it. But hooking up a mini-fridge like this makes lagering beer practically painless. Plug the fridge into the controller, and plug the controller into the wall. Tape the controller's built-in thermometer inside the fridge and set the controller for lagering temperature (55°F for primary fermentation, 40°F for a one-month-long secondary fermentation). That's it! The controller will turn the fridge on and off as needed to hit and maintain the temperature you set. You can find a used fridge cheap, but you'll have to buy the controller from a homebrew store or catalog. They run between $60 and $100.

② RUBBER STOPPER

Most gallon jugs have a 1⅛-inch opening, but check yours to be sure. This corresponds to a #6½ stopper.

③ SCALES

You'll need two: a kitchen scale that can measure from one ounce to five pounds when you're weighing out grain, and a gram scale that can measure smaller amounts (from one to 30 grams) when you're dealing with hops and spices. Scales are usually labeled with their range, something like: 8000 g x 1 g. If you don't have either, you can approximate grain measurements by volume and hops measurements by area. See inside front cover.

④ SPOONS

A nice, solid wooden spoon is indispensable for sloshing around your mash and stirring down a boil. Even professional brewers' mash paddles are basically giant wooden spoons. We modified ours into a dipstick. Fill your brew pot a quart at a time, sticking the spoon in, and cutting a notch in the handle at each incremental waterline. That way, you can easily eyeball how much wort you have in the pot without getting out the measuring cup.

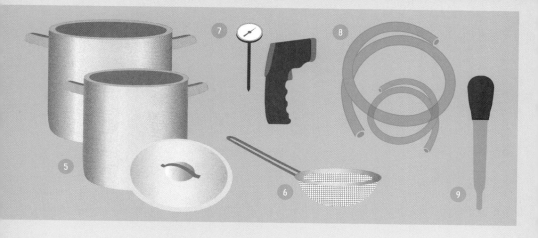

5 STOCKPOTS

We love the double-boiler mashing technique, but it means, of course, you need two pots. We use a large three-gallon pot and a smaller two-gallon pot (with lid) that nests inside. Stuck with one? Don't worry about it, as long as it's big enough to hold two gallons with room to spare. Boil-overs are easy (and sticky) ways to ruin a brew day. As for material, aluminum and stainless steel are best, but chlorine sanitizers can corrode them over time, so use bleach sparingly. Enamel works, too, as long as it's not chipped. Copper pots are as expensive as they are beautiful. They're traditional, and, in fact, copper adds minerals to your beer that yeast loves, but they're not necessary.

6 STRAINER

You need something with mesh that's fine enough to strain out silty trub. Metal strainers are easiest to sanitize. We like using a super-fine-mesh gold coffee filter.

7 THERMOMETER

Any will do, but glass ones break so we like metal. We use an infrared thermometer to quickly check the temperature of our fermenters—with no chance of contamination.

8 TUBES

You'll need two: a wide tube (1-inch inside diameter) to use as a blow-off hose and a narrow one (⅜-inch inside diameter), which you'll connect to your racking cane and use for siphoning beer. These will get dirty fast, and are a pain to clean, so replace them every 5 to 10 batches. Any homebrew shop will stock them, but you can also find them at most hardware stores. Make sure to get clear, food-grade vinyl.

9 TURKEY BASTER

This helps you grab quick samples of fermenting beer to taste or to take a gravity reading. Just be sure the neck is small enough to fit inside your fermenter.

BREW RECORDS

BEER NAME

STYLE

BREWED BY

BREW DATE

GRAIN BILL

	INGREDIENT (MALTS AND OTHER GRAINS)	AMOUNT (wt)
BASE MALTS		
SPECIALTY MALTS		
ADJUNCTS		
	TOTAL WEIGHT	LB

① MASH

CALCULATE YOUR STRIKE WATER QUANTITY BASED ON THE TOTAL WEIGHT OF YOUR GRAIN BILL. HEAT YOUR STRIKE WATER TO YOUR DESIRED MASH TEMPERATURE + 10°F.

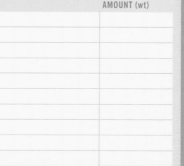

MEASURE AND RECORD YOUR MASH TEMPERATURE

TEMPERATURE (°F): 160° 158 156 154 152 150° 148 146 144 142 140°

TIME (MINUTES): 0 15 30 45 60

LB × 2 QT/LB = QT

AT °F

② SPARGE

COLLECT 2 GALLONS TOTAL WORT

PRE-BOIL GRAVITY:

③ BOIL

	INGREDIENT (HOPS, SPICES, AND SUGAR ADDITIONS)	ALPHA ACID (%)	AMOUNT (g)	BOIL TIME (min)
BITTERING				
FLAVOR				
AROMA				
OTHER				
		TOTAL HOPS		g

④ CHILL

ORIGINAL GRAVITY:

⑤ FERMENT

MEASURE GRAVITY AND TEMPERATURE EVERY FEW DAYS, ESPECIALLY IF AND WHEN YOU DRY-HOP, ADD FRUIT, OR RACK TO A SECONDARY FERMENTER

RECORD BREW DATE, SECONDARY FERMENTATION (IF APPLICABLE), BOTTLING DATE, AND TASTINGS

YEAST STRAIN	AMT. PITCHED	TARGET TEMP.	FERMENTATION TIME

DATE	TEMP (°F)	GRAVITY	ADDITION (HOPS, SUGAR, FRUIT)

FINAL GRAVITY:

Brew Calendar

S	M	T	W	TH	F	SA

⑥ BOTTLE

BOTTLING SUGAR: ____ g   BOTTLE TYPE:

TASTING NOTES

■ HOMEBREWED   ■ COMMERCIAL

BEER NAME	STYLE
BREWED BY	TASTING DATE

AROMA
TEXTURE
FLAVOR IMPRESSIONS
FINISH

APPEARANCE

SERVING STYLE

COLOR

SPECS

BREW DATE
% ABV
ORIGINAL GRAVITY
INGREDIENTS

RATING

SWEETNESS

BITTERNESS

ORIGINALITY

OVERALL RATING

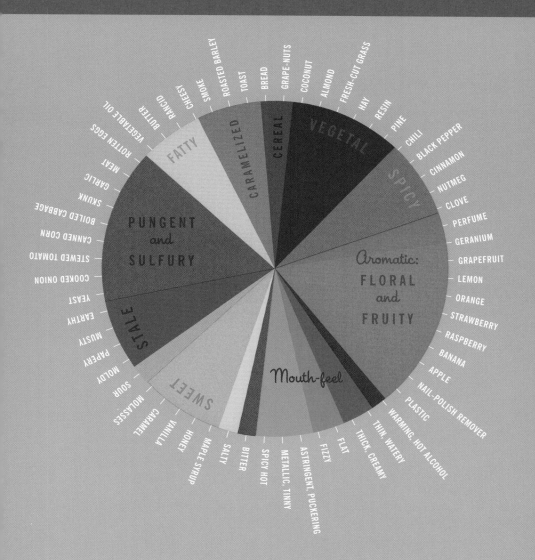

FOR MORE, GO TO BEERCRAFTBOOK.COM

ACETALDEHYDE Chemical with a green-apple aroma common in young, under-fermented beers

ACETOBACTER Souring bacteria with a vinegary bite (acetic acid) common in Flanders red beers

ACIDULATED MALT Malted barley with lactic acid added. Used to make slightly sour beers like Berliner weisse

ADJUNCT GRAIN Grains other than malted barley added to a beer, like corn or rice

AERATE To shake up your wort after pitching yeast, to help get a quick fermentation

ALDEHYDE A precursor to alcohol produced by yeast during fermentation

ALE In the old days, unhopped beer. Today, any beer made with a warm-fermenting ale yeast

ALPHA ACID The bitter component of hop resins

AROMA HOPS Delicate hops added late in a boil to contribute lots of aromatic oils and low levels of bitterness

ATTENUATION How efficiently a yeast eats the sugars in wort

AUTOLYSIS The last stage in a yeast life cycle in which yeast cannibalizes dead cells and releases off flavors

BASE MALT Pale or lightly kilned malted barley used to provide most of the starches, and starch-to-sugar converting enzymes, in a beer

BITTERING HOPS Strong hops added early in a boil to contribute lots of bitter acids and minimal aroma

BOTTLING SUGAR Sugar added to fermented beer at bottling time to give the dormant yeast just enough food to carbonate the bottles. Also called priming sugar

BREAK (HOT, COLD) Proteins that coagulate and settle out during wort boiling or chilling

BRETTANOMYCES A strain of wild yeast discovered in soured British porter

CARAMEL MALT See Crystal malt

CARBOY A glass jug used as a fermenter

CHILL HAZE Cloudiness in a refrigerated beer caused by suspended proteins

CHLOROPHENOL Chemical compound produced by chlorine-based sanitizers

CONDITIONING Aging lagers and stronger beers, sometimes at cooler temperatures, to mellow their flavors

CRAFT BREWERY Any independently owned brewery producing fewer than two million barrels of beer per year using traditional methods

CRYSTAL MALT Malted barley heated while wet to liquefy and caramelize the starches inside. Comes in a range of colors and sweetnesses. Also called Caramel malt

DECOCTION A complicated mashing process involving removing, boiling, and reintroducing small amounts of grain

DEXTRINS Sugars produced during a mash that can't be fermented by brewing yeast and that make for a sweeter beer

DIACETYL A by-product of fermentation common as an off flavor in young lagers

DIACETYL REST Briefly raising the temperature of a fermenting lager before cold-conditioning to help clean up diacetyl flavors

DIASTATIC POWER A measure of the number of enzymes in a malt, and how easily they will convert the starches to sugars

DIMETHYL SULFIDE A chemical produced by wort-spoiling bacteria in infected beer

DRY-HOPPING Adding hops to beer while it conditions to amplify hop aroma

DUAL-USE HOPS Hops added in the middle of a boil to contribute both bittering acids and aromatic oils. Also called flavoring hops

ENZYME Compounds in malt that turn starches into fermentable sugars

ESTER Fruity chemical compounds produced by yeasts during high-temperature fermentations

FERMENTATION The process by which yeast turns sugars into alcohol and carbon dioxide

FIRST RUNNINGS The very sweet wort drained out of a mash before rinsing or sparging

FIRST-WORT HOPPING Adding hops to wort as it comes to a boil to amplify aromatic hop notes

FLAVORING HOPS See dual-use hops

FLAVOR MALT Barley malt kilned a bit hotter than base malt to produce sweeter, toasty aromas and flavors

FLOCCULATION When yeast finishes fermenting, clumps together, and settles out of beer

GELATINIZATION Unlocking starches in unmalted grains like rice by cooking them before adding to a mash

GRAVITY A measure of the amount of sugars dissolved in a beer; the higher the gravity, the stronger and sweeter the beer

HARD WATER Water with a lot of dissolved minerals

HOPBACK A container of hops or other spices through which brewers may pour wort to flavor it

HYDROMETER A tool used for measuring the specific gravity, or density, of a liquid

IBU International Bittering Units, a measure of bitterness in beer

IRISH MOSS A kind of seaweed used by some brewers to help proteins settle out in a wort after it has boiled

ISOMERIZE To dissolve hops' bitter acids in wort by boiling

KILN To heat malted grains after they sprout in order to dry them and stop their growth

KRAEUSEN The layer of foam produced by fermenting yeast

LACTIC ACID A sour acid common in Flanders reds, browns, and lambics

LACTOBACILLUS A strain of wild bacteria that produces sour lactic acid

LAGER To condition or secondary-ferment a beer at cold temperatures (usually around 40°F) for a few weeks to a few months. Lager also refers to any beer made this way

LATE-HOPPING Adding hops very late in a boil to preserve their oils and amplify their aromatic notes

LIGHTSTRUCK Beer degraded by sunlight, which produces skunklike aromas

LOVIBOND A measurement of malt color, listed in degrees

LUPULIN GLANDS Small yellow packets of bitter resins and aromatic oils found in hop cones

MALT Barley grains that have just started to sprout and unlock their starches

MALT EXTRACT A wort of malted barley that has been partially or completely evaporated, leaving behind a syrup or powder of pre-converted malt sugars

MALTOSE One of the sugars produced in a mash when enzymes convert the starches in malted barley

MASH Mixing malted grains with hot water to turn their starches into sugar

MODIFICATION A measure of the amount and accessibility of starches in a malt

NOBLE HOPS A few German and Czech varieties prized for their light bitterness and subtle aroma

OXIDATION The degradation of hop flavor molecules during storage

pH A measure of acidity in a liquid

PEDIOCOCCUS Souring bacteria common in lambics

PHENOL Sharp off-flavor compounds produced in beer by bacterial infection or mash tannins

PITCH To add yeast to your wort

PRIMARY FERMENTATION The most active stage of brewing yeast's life cycle, in which most of the sugars in a wort are converted to alcohol and carbon dioxide

PRIME To mix a bit of sugar in with your beer when bottling, to carbonate

RACK To transfer beer or wort from one vessel to another with a long tube

REINHEITSGEBOT Germany's beer purity law, limiting beer's ingredients to water, malt, hops, and yeast

ROASTED MALT Dark, flavorful malt toasted very hot to brown or burn its starches

SACCHARIFICATION Enzyme activity in a mash that turns malt starches into fermentable sugars

SACCHAROMYCES The strain of yeast most commonly used for brewing

SECOND RUNNINGS The slightly less-sweet wort drained out of mashed grains after rinsing or sparging

SECONDARY FERMENTATION A long aging period for stronger beers in which they're separated from the yeast after fermentation and transferred to a clean fermenter

SIPHON To move beer from one vessel to another using gravity and air pressure

SMACK PACK Yeast packaging used by Wyeast, in which a small pouch of wort is broken inside a larger pouch of yeast to wake up the cells

SOFT WATER Water free of most minerals

SOUR BEER A beer partially or completely fermented by wild bacteria, which produce sour flavors. Flanders reds, browns, and lambics are common versions of the style

SPARGE To rinse mashed grains with water and extract their last remaining sugars

SPENT GRAINS Malt that has been mashed, drained, and rinsed of all its sugars

SPECIFIC GRAVITY A measure of the dissolved sugars and potential alcohol content in beer or wort

STARCH A precursor to sugar produced in barley during the malting process and converted to sugar by enzymes in a mash

STARTER A small colony of yeast grown to a large enough size to pitch into wort

TANNIN Bitter chemicals in grains that can be leached into wort when overheated

TRUB Sediment of grain husks, hop particles, proteins, and yeast cells that collects after boiling and fermentation

WET-HOPPING Using undried, unprocessed hops straight from the vine

WORT (pronounced "wert") Sweet, unfermented liquid made from steeping malted grains in hot water

BEER CRAFT

For more recipes, links to suppliers, video tutorials, and more, find us at:

beercraftbook.com

twitter.com/beercraftbook

closedmondays.org

SUPPLIES

Midwest Supplies
midwestsupplies.com

MoreBeer
morebeer.com

Northern Brewer
nothernbrewer.com

ORGANIZATIONS

American Homebrewers Association
homebrewersassociation.org

Beer Judge Certification Program
bjcp.org

Brewers Association
brewersassociation.org
craftbeer.com

MAGAZINES

BeerAdvocate

Brew Your Own

Draft

Zymurgy

BOOKS

RECIPES

Brewing Classic Styles
Jamil Zainasheff and John Palmer

The Complete Joy of Homebrewing
Charlie Papazian

Designing Great Beers
Ray Daniels

How to Brew
John Palmer

ADVANCED TECHNIQUES

Brew Ware
Karl F. Lutzen and Mark Stevens

Farmhouse Ales
Phil Markowski

Radical Brewing
Randy Mosher

Sacred and Herbal Healing Beers
Stephen Harrod Buhner

Wild Brews
Jeff Sparrow

TASTING AND PAIRING

The Brewmaster's Table
Garrett Oliver

Tasting Beer
Randy Mosher

HISTORY

Brewed in America
Stanley Baron

A Revolution in Eating
James E. McWilliams

DESIGN

US Beer Labels (all volumes)
Bob Kay

WEBSITES

TASTING AND RATING BEER

BeerAdvocate
beeradvocate.com

RateBeer
ratebeer.com

BEER SAMPLE TESTING

Analysis Laboratory
analysislaboratory.com

LABELS, CAPS, AND BREWERIANA

All Over Beer
flickr.com/alloverbeer

American Breweriana Association
americanbreweriana.org

Bob Kay Beer Labels, Inc.
home.comcast.net/~beerlabel/

Bottle Cap Man
thebottlecapman.com

Crowncap Collectors Society Intl.
bottlecapclub.org

ACKNOWLEDGMENTS

Brewing, like drinking, goes better with friends, and we couldn't have made this book—or the beer in it—without ours. First, we'd like to thank all the brewers who welcomed us on our travels, sharing their work, advice, and the occasional six pack: C.V. Howe and Andy Parker at Avery; Christopher Basso at Brooklyn Brewery; Tyler King and Benjamin Weiss at The Bruery; Dave Engbers at Founders; Chris Davis, Brooks Hamaker, and Sean Lilly Wilson at Fullsteam; Patrick Langlois and Taylor Rees at Great Divide; Sarah Russell at Great Lakes Brewing; Ron Jeffries and Charles Psenka at Jolly Pumpkin; Bret and Eric Kuhnhenn at Kuhnhenn; Ron Lindenbusch and Jeremy Marshall at Lagunitas; Lauren Salazar and Bryan Simpson at New Belgium; Larry Bennett and Phil Leinhart at Ommegang; Brett Joyce and John Maier at Rogue; Ken Grossman and Bill Manley at Sierra Nevada; Shane C. Welch at Sixpoint; Greg Koch, Jacob McKean, and Karen Westfall at Stone; and John Trogner at Tröegs.

Thanks also to Duncan Bock, Bonnie Eldon, Lia Ronnen, and our agent, Devin McIntyre, for helping us turn an idea into a book; to Avril and David Bright, Lori Baker Brown and David Brown, Jim, Dawn, Silas, and Beatrice Hammel, Mary Hicks, Rafe Judkins, Frank Santoro, and Tobias Womack, for giving us a place to write this thing; and Jim Egan and Brett Martin for their advice on how to write it. To our photographer, Jeff Elkins. To Barbara Gogan, Parlan McGaw, Amélie Cherlin, Kathleen Barber, James Tyler, and Gena Smith for their editorial help—and especially Colin Dickerman, who humored us even though when it comes to beer he drinks only Presidente. To Lex Leifheit and Dan McKinley, for letting us use their wedding to try out a recipe, and all the brave taste-testers of good batches and bad: Dan Bornstein, Daniel del Valle, Joanna Epstein, Alissa Faden, Henry Julier, J.D. Nasaw, Regine Raab, Dave Rivello, Dan Rosenbaum, Justin Spindler, Emily Turner, Amy Van Arsdale, Rebecca Wiener, and Carl Williamson. Love and thanks, most of all, to our parents and grandparents—our first editors, best publicists, and most enthusiastic tasters—for everything.

Photography by **Jeff Elkins**, jeffelkinsphoto.com

Book design and illustrations by **Jessi Rymill**, Closed Mondays

Custom lettering by **Jeremy Mickel**

Vintage labels courtesy **Bob Kay** (home.comcast.net/~beerlabel) and **Brian Stechschulte** (alloverbeer.com)

Copyedited by **Barbara Gogan**

Proofread by **Amélie Cherlin** and **Parlan McGaw**

Indexed by **Kathleen Barber**

We inspire and enable people to improve their lives and the world around them.
www.rodalebooks.com